SELECTED WRITINGS ON CLIENT CENTERED THERAPY

Selected Writings on Client Centered Therapy

Selected Writings of Carl Rogers, Including:

Becoming a Person
Significant Aspects of Client Centered Therapy
The Process of Therapy
&
The Development of Insight in a Counseling
Relationship

by

Carl R. Rogers, Ph.D.

MOCKINGBIRD
PRESS

Cover, "Inner World," by Paul Craft, Used under license from Shutterstock, Inc.,
ID # 1719414886.
Cover Design by Jenny Frank, Copyright © 2021 Mockingbird Press
Interior Design by Maria Johnson
Foreword by Mary Beck, Copyright © 2021 Mockingbird Press

Publisher's Cataloging-In-Publication Data

Rogers, Carl, author; with Mary Beck, foreword by.
Selected Writings On Client Centered Therapy : Becoming a Person, Significant
Aspects of Client Centered Therapy, The Process of Therapy, & The Development
of Insight in a Counseling Relationship.

Paperback	ISBN-13: 978-1-953450-78-4
Hardback	ISBN-13: 978-1-953450-79-1
Ebook	ISBN-13: 978-1-953450-80-7

1. Psychology—Clinical Psychology. 2. Society & Social Sciences—Psychology I.
Author Carl Rogers. II. Foreword by Mary Beck. III. Selected Writings on Client
Centered Therapy. IV. Title : Becoming a Person, Significant Aspects of Client
Centered Therapy, The Process of Therapy, & The Development of Insight in a
Counseling Relationship.

PSY007000 / JM

Type Set in Schoolbook / **Franklin Gothic Demi**

Mockingbird Press, Augusta, GA

CONTENTS

FOREWORD

IN many ways, Carl Rogers was a revolutionary. Raised in a strict, conservative home, Rogers eventually developed a theory of psychology that swept away old power structures and put the patient in charge of his own treatment. His work continues to be important for what it teaches us about relationships and human potential, as well as about psychology.

Unlike earlier practitioners of psychology, like Sigmund Freud or Carl Jung, Rogers did not elaborate a unifying theory of human consciousness. His work is not focused on unconscious drives, collective memory, or hidden impulses. It does not dwell on childhood memories or on sexuality, unless the patient (or, to use Rogers' own word, the client) wants to dwell on those matters.

Instead, Rogers focused on what he called the desire for self-actualization. He believed that by creating the right conditions, therapy could release people from whatever was holding them back so that they could discover their true selves and live in harmony with the world around them.

* * *

Rogers is probably best known for developing what he called nondirective, or client-centered therapy. He argued that people were innately good and possessed the ability to heal themselves, even when they had become seriously disconnected from reality. However, this sort of healing couldn't occur in a vacuum. Rogers stressed the importance of therapeutic relationships to give people the confidence and freedom to develop, so that they could achieve their true potential.

Rogers assigned therapists a different role than the one they'd traditionally had. Traditionally, analysts had taken a fairly active role in their patients' treatment, offering their opinions on patients' needs

1

and progress. Under Rogers' system, though, therapists took on a more passive position. Rather than diagnosing their patients or presenting a treatment plan, therapists focused on creating an atmosphere of warmth, safety, and acceptance.

Rogers' ideal therapist was not a detached authority figure, taking notes while his patient poured out his earliest childhood memories. Rather, Rogers wanted therapists to enter into a genuine relationship with their clients. This would give clients the space they needed to drop their masks and gradually confront their true personhood.

* * *

Rogers wrote extensively about the difference between his therapeutic approach and older approaches. The traditional psychologist-centered approach, he argued, was bound to be problematic. Its top-down method did not give patients space to really understand their own fears and blind spots, or to come to terms with the kinds of changes they needed to make in their lives. Rogers writes, "It is possible to explain a person to himself, to prescribe steps which should lead him forward, to train him in knowledge about a more satisfying mode of life. But such methods are, in my experience, futile and inconsequential."

The top-down method is futile, Rogers explained, because whatever insights the therapist presented to his client would not really sink in. If a person is to truly integrate a new set of ideas, he must be ready for them—which often means that he must come to those ideas on his own, after a long period of gradually letting down his defenses.

That is why the client-centered approach begins with a relationship, as Rogers explains: "If I can provide a certain type of relationship, the other person will discover within himself the capacity to use that relationship for growth, and change and personal development will occur." The ideal relationship is one of absolute acceptance in which clients could feel safe and secure enough to begin exploring their full selves— not just the narrow, restricted persona they might present to the world, but a fuller and more adaptable self.

* * *

How did Carl Rogers arrive at his beliefs? What forces and influences went into creating the man who developed client-centered therapy?

Rogers was born in a suburb of Chicago, Illinois, in 1902. He was the fourth child of six in a middle class family; his father was a civil engineer, and his mother was a housewife. The family was devoutly Christian and had a strongly conservative bent, which Rogers does not appear to have questioned.

When the young Carl was just 12, the family moved to a rural area, and Carl developed an interest in farming. He eventually attended the University of Wisconsin at Madison, majoring in agriculture with a concentration in religion. He later moved to New York City to attend Union Theological Seminary, planning to become a pastor.

At some point, whether at seminary himself or while on a trip to a Christian conference in China, Carl suffered a crisis of faith. He underwent a gradual shift in focus, moving away from religion but continuing to wish to minister to his fellow man. He transferred from the seminary to Columbia University's Teachers College, where he took courses in psychology. Finally he graduated with an MA in education and a PhD in psychology.

* * *

Rogers' first job after graduation was as a child psychologist. While still completing his dissertation, he had become involved with the Society for the Prevention of Cruelty to Children in Rochester, New York. He went on to work with the Society full time, becoming the director of the organization. His first book, "The Clinical Treatment of the Problem Child," grew out of his work with the Society and focused on the ways that a child's environment, socialization, and economic circumstances could impact behavioral issues.

Rogers went on to take a job as professor at Ohio State University and to develop his ideas further. In 1942, he wrote "Counseling and Psychotherapy: Newer Concepts in Practice," which was designed to introduce the public to his methods and principles. The book was revolutionary for its focus on the individual, rather than on the therapist.

In 1945, he moved to Chicago to open a counseling center at the University of Chicago, and a few years later he published his book, "Client-Centered Therapy." Several years later, he was appointed president of the American Academy of Psychotherapists. He spent a few years at the University of Wisconsin before moving to La Jolla, California, to serve on the staff of the Western Behavioral Sciences Institute.

Unlike many psychologists, Rogers took an active interest in politics and in the world around him. He worked closely with parties to the conflicts in South Africa and in Northern Ireland (he has also described his own difficulty in achieving a good working relationship with members of the South African army, given his own qualms about their behavior). Rogers was nominated for the Nobel Peace Prize for his work on international conflict. He passed away at the age of 85 in 1987, the same year that he was nominated for the award.

* * *

The works contained in this volume give a rich view of Rogers' principles. They are written in Rogers' typical accessible, engaging style; they are more like conversation than lectures.

They also give us some insight into how Rogers came by those principles. Careful readers will notice that Rogers was influenced by the likes of Soren Kierkegaard, especially when it came to the ongoing search for self. Rogers quotes Kierkegaard as saying, "to will to be that self which one truly is, is indeed the opposite of despair."

The work titled "Becoming a Person: the Facilitation of Personal Growth" builds on that idea—the search for the self in combination with the quest for happiness—and applies it to the central problem of the psychologist, namely, what to do when faced with a troubled, conflicted person who is seeking and expecting help. For Rogers, each patient has the same problem—who am I, really? How can I become myself? The successful psychologist can help his clients to answer that question. And by answering the question and finding their true selves, patients can reorganize their lives and their relationship to society, finding the satisfaction that had eluded them.

Rogers argues that in a "suitable psychological climate," characterized by a mood of companionship and transparency, individuals will be able to understand what is causing them pain and suffering, and then reorganize their personalities and their relationship to life. Under the influence of a good relationship, Rogers wrote, individuals are able to shed their neurotic qualities, value themselves more highly, relate better to others, and find more common ground with their fellows.

It's not all about the relationship, of course. In Rogers' view, the therapist merely provides the right atmosphere—it is the client who does the real work of uncovering the true self. This entails a long and often slow process of peeling away the "masks" that disguise the true self, and facing up to all of the buried emotions that have been trapped within. The task is onerous, but the reward, Rogers promises, is great:

"When a person has, throughout therapy, experienced in this fashion all the emotions which organismically arise in him . . . then he has experienced himself, in all the richness that exists within himself."

The person who emerges from this therapeutic experience is renewed, in all sorts of ways. They are, Rogers writes, more open to the reality of his experience, where previously he may have been defensive and rigid. They are able to take in the evidence of a new situation as it truly is, rather than distorting it to fit a pattern which he already holds. They are also newly able to tolerate ambiguity and to cope with conflicting evidence, without trying to force premature conclusions.

In other words, he has been reborn, stronger and more flexible than ever before.

* * *

In "Significant Aspects of Client-Centered Therapy," Rogers details the process of successful therapy. The work contains fascinating excerpts from therapy sessions conducted by Rogers and his colleagues. It also contains excerpts from less successful sessions conducted by psychology-centered therapists.

Rogers explains his views on the importance of insight in the counseling relationship. It should never be imposed by the psychologist—rather, the psychologist or therapist should always ask themselves, how may this individual come to an effective understanding of himself?

Although every individual is unique, the therapeutic relationship follows a certain fixed pattern. There is, Rogers explains, the "experience of release," when the patient loosens their internal bonds and pours out the feelings which had been trapped inside. This is followed by an insight into the Self, and then by the formation of a new plan for a better life—a new and more satisfactory way for the Self to adjust to reality.

These three stages must be reached organically, without pressure from the therapist. Rogers notes that "most of the procedures which we customarily use in counseling tend to put the client subtly on his guard." Even simple, positive remarks like "you're right" or "I agree with you" can set up a hierarchical relationship, implying that the therapist ultimately knows best and is in a position to approve or disapprove. Ultimately, this will put the client on the defensive, which slows or prevents the experience of release.

The answer, Rogers argues, is for the therapist to limit themself to just two basic techniques: simple acceptance, and mirroring. Mirroring, or repeating the client's concerns back to him, conveys a sense of understanding without judgement, positive or negative. So does simple acceptance.

"Significant Aspects of Client-Centered Therapy" also sets out what Rogers calls his "heretical" conclusions, namely, that training and practice in therapy is more important than diagnostic training, and should precede it. He argues that diagnostic knowledge is not needed at all for good therapy to take place—in fact, diagnostics can derail the therapeutic relationship, by putting the client on guard and making them feel, anxiously, that they are being assessed.

* * *

By skipping over diagnostics and focusing on the relationship, the client-centered approach opens up new avenues of possibility and exploration of the self. One of the pleasures in reading Carl Rogers is in tracing the reach of his influence today.

Other psychologists, too, have been influenced by Rogers' ideas. One of his best-known students is probably Eugene Gendlin, who went on to found the Focusing Institute. It is easy to see the link between his "felt sense" and Rogers' therapeutic release of emotions; both are closely followed by insights which derive from the client, rather than from the therapist.

But Gendlin isn't the only one to reflect Rogers' theories. Our society's views on parenting, for example, have been forever marked by his belief in the value of unconditional love and acceptance. In a way, the self-help movement, which empowers ordinary people to treat their own conditions, builds on Rogers' work.

That's why it's so important to read the great thinker's works, as he wrote them.

Becoming a Person

Two Lectures Delivered On The Nellie Heldt Lecture Fund

by

Carl R. Rogers, Ph.D.

Professor of Psychology
and
Executive Secretary, Counseling Center
University of Chicago

THE NELLIE HELDT
LECTURE FUND

The Nellie Heldt Lecture Fund was given to Oberlin College by Dr. and Mrs. Thomas J. Heldt and their children in memory of their daughter and sister, Nellie Rosa Heldt, who had been a student in Oberlin College from 1929 to 1932. The income of the Fund is used "to provide an annual or biennial lecture or lectures during the academic year on some humanitarian or scientific subject which may be deemed important to the time."

FOREWORD TO BECOMING A PERSON

THESE lectures were presented as the major part of a Symposium on Emotional Development in College. The Symposium was conceived and executed by a group of students from several fields interested in problems of maladjustment. The purpose of the Symposium as it developed in many committee meetings over a period of six months was not so much to achieve some particular socio-institutional goal as to stimulate thought and discussion on a basic social and personal problem.

Dr. Rogers' experience in counseling is extensive. He is the founder of an orientation in psychotherapy widely known as client-centered therapy, and he has written several books on clinical psychology and counseling. But Dr. Rogers' experience and conclusions apply not alone to the admittedly limited professionally therapeutic situation. They have a broader significance for human relations in general, so that his remarks are extremely relevant for an audience with little or no knowledge of psychology. It is this audience the Symposium was designed to reach. Before an assembly of the college, Dr. Rogers spoke of some of the conditions, processes, and results of the particular sort of helping relationship involved in his method of therapy, and dealt with some of its applications to other human relationships such as parent-child or teacher-student relationships. In an evening talk he emphasized what it means to become more fully integrated, to find oneself, to fulfill the basic search which lies below the level of the situation against which the individual is protesting.

Rufus P. Browning
Chairman of the Symposium.

SOME HYPOTHESES REGARDING
THE FACILITATION OF PERSONAL GROWTH

To be faced by a troubled, conflicted person who is seeking and expecting help, has always constituted a great challenge to me. Do I have the knowledge, the resources, the psychological strength, the skill—do I have whatever it takes to be of help to such an individual?

For more than twenty-five years I have been trying to meet this kind of challenge. It has caused me to draw upon every element of my professional background: the rigorous methods of personality measurement which I first learned at Teachers College, Columbia; the Freudian psychoanalytic insights and methods of the Institute for Child Guidance where I worked as intern; the continuing developments in the field of clinical psychology, with which I have been closely associated; the briefer exposure to the work of Otto Rank, the methods of psychiatric social work, and other contacts too numerous to mention. But most of all it has meant a continual learning from my own experience and that of my colleagues at the Counseling Center as we have endeavored to discover for ourselves effective means of working with people in distress. Gradually I have developed a way of working which grows out of that experience, and which can be tested, refined, and reshaped by further experience and by research.

One brief way of describing the change which has taken place in me is to say that in my early professional years I was asking the question: How can I treat, or cure, or change this person? Now I would phrase the question this way: How can I provide a relationship which this person may use for his own personal growth?

It is as I have come to put the question in this second way that I realize that whatever I have learned is applicable to all of my human relationships, not just to working with clients with problems. It is for this reason that I feel it is possible that the learnings which have had meaning for me in my experience may have some meaning for you in your experience, since all of us are involved in human relationships.

Perhaps I should start with a negative learning. It has gradually been driven home to me that I cannot be of help to this troubled person by means of any intellectual or training procedure. No approach which relies upon knowledge, upon training, upon the acceptance of something that is taught, is of any use. These approaches seem so tempting and direct that I have, in the past, tried a great many of them. It is possible to explain a person to himself, to prescribe steps which should lead him forward, to train him in knowledge about a more satisfying mode of life. But such methods are, in my experience, futile and inconsequential. The most they can accomplish is some temporary change, which soon disappears, leaving the individual more than ever convinced of his inadequacy.

The failure of any such approach through the intellect has forced me to recognize that change appears to come about through experience in a relationship. So I am going to try to state very briefly and informally some of the essential hypotheses regarding a helping relationship which have seemed to gain increasing confirmation both from experience and research.

I can state the overall hypothesis in one sentence, as follows. If I can provide a certain type of relationship, the other person will discover within himself the capacity to use that relationship for growth, and change and personal development will occur.

But what meaning do these terms have? Let me take separately the three major phrases in this sentence and indicate something of the meaning they have for me. What is this certain type of relationship I would like to provide?

I have found that the more I can be genuine in the relationship, the more helpful it will be. This means that I need to be aware of my own feelings, in so far as possible, rather than presenting an outward facade of one attitude, while actually holding another attitude at a deeper or unconscious level. Being genuine also involves the willingness to be and to express, in my words and my behavior, the various feelings and attitudes which exist in me. It is only in this way that the relationship can have reality, and reality seems deeply important as a first condition. It is only by providing the genuine reality which is in me, that the other person can successfully seek for the reality in him.

As a second condition, I find that the more acceptance and liking I feel toward this individual, the more I will be creating a relationship which he can use. By acceptance I mean a warm regard for him as a person of unconditional self-worth—of value no matter what his condition, his behavior, or his feelings. It means a respect and liking for him as a separate person, a willingness for him to possess his own feelings in his own way. It means an acceptance of and regard for his attitudes of the moment, no matter how negative or positive, no matter how much they may contradict other attitudes he has held in the past. This acceptance of each fluctuating aspect of this other person makes it for him a relationship of warmth and safety, and the safety of being liked and prized as a person seems a highly important element in a helping relationship.

I also find that the relationship is significant to the extent that I feel a continuing desire to understand—a sensitive empathy with each of the client's feelings and communications as they seem to him at that moment. Acceptance does not mean much until it involves understanding. It is only as I understand the feelings and thoughts which seem so horrible to you, or so weak, or so sentimental, or so bizarre—it is only as I see them as you see them, and accept them and you, that you can feel really free to explore all the hidden nooks and frightening crannies of your inner and often buried experience. This freedom is an important condition of the relationship. There is implied here a freedom to explore oneself at both conscious and unconscious levels, as rapidly as one can dare to embark on this dangerous quest. There is also a complete freedom from any type of moral or diagnostic evaluation, since all such evaluations are, I believe, always threatening.

Thus the relationship which I have found helpful is characterized by a sort of transparency on my part, in which my real feelings are evident; by an acceptance of this other person as a separate person with value in his own right; and by a deep empathic understanding which enables me to see his private world through his eyes. When these conditions are achieved, I become a companion to my client, accompanying him in the frightening search for himself, which he now feels free to undertake.

I am by no means always able to achieve this kind of relationship with another, and sometimes, even when I feel I have achieved it in myself, he may be too frightened to perceive what is being offered to him. But I would say that when I hold in myself the kind of attitudes I have described, and when the other person can to some degree experience these attitudes, then I believe that change and constructive personal development will invariably occur—and I include that word "invariably" only after long and careful consideration.

So much for the relationship. The second phrase in my overall hypothesis was that the individual will discover within himself the capacity to use this relationship for growth. I will try to indicate something of the meaning which that phrase has for me. Gradually my experience has forced me to conclude that the individual has within himself the capacity and the tendency, latent if not evident, to move forward toward maturity. In a suitable psychological climate this tendency is released and becomes actual rather than potential. It is evident in the capacity of the individual to understand those aspects of his life and of himself which are causing him pain and dissatisfaction, an understanding which probes beneath his conscious knowledge of himself into those experiences which he has hidden from himself because of their threatening nature. It shows itself in the tendency to reorganize his personality and his relationship to life in ways which are regarded as more mature. Whether one calls it a growth tendency, a drive toward self-actualization, or a forward-moving directional tendency, it is the mainspring of life, and is, in the last analysis, the tendency upon which all psychotherapy depends. It is the urge which is evident in all organic and human life—to expand, extend, become autonomous, develop, mature—the tendency to express and activate all the capacities of the organism, to the extent that such activation enhances the organism or the self. This tendency may become deeply buried under layer after layer of encrusted psychological defenses; it may be hidden behind elaborate facades which deny its existence; but it is my belief that it exists in every individual, and awaits only the proper conditions to be released and expressed.

I have attempted to describe the relationship which is basic to constructive personality change. I have tried to put into words the type of capacity which the individual brings to such a relationship. The third phrase of my general statement was that change and personal development would occur. It is my hypothesis that in such a relationship the individual will reorganize himself at both the conscious and deeper levels of his personality in such a manner as to cope with life more constructively, more intelligently, and in a more socialized as well as a more satisfying way.

Here I can depart from speculation and bring in the steadily increasing body of solid research knowledge which is accumulating. We know now that individuals who live in such a relationship even for a relatively limited number of hours show profound and significant changes in personality, attitudes, and behavior, changes that do not occur in matched control groups. In such a relationship the individual becomes more integrated, more effective. He shows fewer of the characteristics which are usually termed neurotic or psychotic, and more of the characteristics of the healthy, well-functioning person. He changes his perception of himself, becoming more realistic in his views of self. He becomes more like the person he wishes to be. He values himself more highly. He is more self-confident and self-directing. He has a better understanding of himself, becomes more open to his experience, denies or represses less of his experience. He becomes more accepting in his attitudes toward others, seeing others as more similar to himself.

In his behavior he shows similar changes. He is less frustrated by stress, and recovers from stress more quickly. He becomes more mature in his everyday behavior as this is observed by friends. He is less defensive, more adaptive, more able to meet situations creatively.

These are some of the changes which we now know come about in individuals who have completed a series of counseling interviews in which the psychological atmosphere approximates the relationship I have described. Each of the statements made is based upon objective evidence. Much more research needs to be done, but there can no longer be any doubt as to the effectiveness of such a relationship in producing personality change.

To me, the exciting thing about these research findings is not simply the fact that they prove the efficacy of one form of psychotherapy, though that is by no means unimportant. The excitement comes from the fact that these findings justify an even broader hypothesis regarding all human relationships. There seems every reason to suppose that the therapeutic relationship is only one instance of interpersonal relations, and the same lawfulness governs all such relationships. Thus it seems reasonable to hypothesize that if the parent creates with his child a psychological climate such as we have described, then the child will become more self-directing, socialized, and mature. To the extent that the teacher creates such a relationship with his class, the student will become a self-initiated learner, more original, more self-disciplined, less anxious, and other-directed. If the administrator, or military or industrial leader, creates such a climate within his organization, then his staff will become more self-responsible, more creative, better able to adapt to new problems, more basically co-operative. It appears possible to me that we are seeing the emergence of a new field of human relationships, in which we may specify that if certain attitudinal conditions exist, then certain definable changes will occur.

Let me conclude by returning to a personal statement. I have tried to share with you something of what I have learned in trying to be of help to troubled, unhappy, maladjusted individuals. I have formulated the hypothesis which has gradually come to have meaning for me—not only in my relationship to clients in distress, but in all my human relationships. I have indicated that such research knowledge as we have supports this hypothesis, but that there is much more investigation needed. I should like now to pull together into one statement the conditions of this general hypothesis and the effects which are specified.

If I can create a relationship characterized on my part:

by a genuineness and transparency, in which I am my real feelings;

by a warm acceptance of and liking for the other person as a separate individual;

by a sensitive ability to see his world and himself as he sees them;

Then the other individual in the relationship:

will experience and understand aspects of himself which previously he has repressed;

will find himself becoming better integrated, more able to function effectively;

will become more similar to the person he would like to be;

will be more self-directing and self-confident;

will become more of a person, more unique, and more self-expressive; will be able to cope with the problems of life more adequately and more comfortably.

I believe that this statement holds whether I am speaking of my relationship with a client, with a group of students or staff members, with my family or children. It seems to me that we have here a general hypothesis which offers exciting possibilities for the development of creative, adaptive, inner-directed persons.

WHAT IT MEANS TO BECOME
A PERSON

A frequently-raised question is: "What problems do people bring to you and other counselors at the Counseling Center?" I always feel baffled by this question. One reply is that they bring every kind of problem one can imagine, and quite a number that I believe no one would imagine. There is the student concerned about failing in college; the housewife disturbed about her marriage; the individual who feels he is teetering on the edge of a complete breakdown or psychosis; the responsible professional man who spends much of his time in sexual fantasies and functions inefficiently in his work; the brilliant student, at the top of his class, who is paralyzed by the conviction that he is hopelessly and helplessly inadequate; the parent who is distressed by his child's behavior; the popular girl who finds herself unaccountably overtaken by sharp spells of black depression; the woman who fears that life and love are passing her by, and that her good graduate record is a poor recompense; the man who has become convinced that powerful and sinister forces are plotting against him;—I could go on and on with the many different and unique problems which people bring to us. They run the gamut of life's experiences. Yet there is no satisfaction in giving this type of catalog, for, as counselor, I know that the problem as stated in the first interview will not be the problem as seen in the second or third hour, and by the tenth interview it will be a still different problem or series of problems. You can see why I feel baffled as to how to answer this simple question.

I have however come to believe that in spite of this bewildering horizontal multiplicity, and the layer upon layer of vertical complexity, there is a simple answer. As I follow the experience of many clients in the therapeutic relationship which we endeavor to create for them, it seems to me that each one has the same problem. Below the level of the problem situation about which the individual is complaining—behind the trouble with studies, or wife, or employer, or with his own uncontrollable or bizarre behavior, or with his frightening feelings, lies one central search. It seems to me that at bottom each person is asking: "Who am I, really? How can I get in touch with this real self, underlying all my surface behavior? How can I become myself?"

The Process of Becoming

Getting Behind the Mask

Let me try to explain what I mean when I say that it appears that the goal the individual most wishes to achieve, the end which he knowingly and unknowingly pursues, is to become himself.

When a person comes to me, troubled by his unique combination of difficulties, I have found it most worthwhile to try to create a relationship with him in which he is safe and free. It is my purpose to understand the way he feels in his own inner world, to accept him as he is, to create an atmosphere of freedom in which he can move in his thinking and feeling and being, in any direction he desires. How does he use this freedom?

It is my experience that he uses it to become more and more himself. He begins to drop the false fronts, or the masks, or the roles, with which he has faced life. He appears to be trying to discover something more basic, something more truly himself. At first he lays aside masks which he is to some degree aware of using. One young woman describes in a counseling interview one of the masks she has been using, and how uncertain she is whether underneath this appeasing, ingratiating front there is any real self with convictions.

I was thinking about this business of standards. I somehow developed a sort of knack, I guess, of—well—a habit—of trying to make people feel at ease around me, or to make things go along smoothly. There always had to be some appeaser around, being sort of the oil that soothed the waters. At a small meeting, or a little party, or something—I could help things go along nicely and appear to be having a good time. And sometimes I'd surprise myself by arguing against what I really thought when I saw that the person in charge would be quite unhappy about it if I didn't. In other words I just wasn't ever—I mean, I didn't find myself ever being set and definite about things. Now the reason why I did it probably was I'd been doing it around home so much. I just didn't stand up for my own convictions, until I don't know whether I have any convictions to stand up for. I haven't been really honestly being myself, or actually knowing what my real self is, and I've been just playing a sort of false role.

You can, in this excerpt, see her examining the mask she has been using, recognizing her dissatisfaction with it, and wondering how to get to the real self underneath, if such a self exists.

In this attempt to discover his own self, the client typically uses the therapeutic relationship to explore, to examine the various aspects of his own experience, to recognize and face up to the deep contradictions which he often discovers. He learns how much of his behavior, even how much of the feeling he experiences, is not real, is not something which flows from the genuine reactions of his organism, but is a facade, a front, behind which he has been hiding. He discovers how much of his life is guided by what he thinks he should be, not by what he is. Often he discovers that he exists only in response to the demands of others, that he seems to have no self of his own, that he is only trying to think, and feel, and behave in the way that others believe he ought to think, and feel, and behave.

In this connection I have been astonished to find how accurately the Danish philosopher, Soren Kierkegaard, pictured the dilemma of the individual more than a century ago, with keen psychological insight. He points out that the most common despair is to be in despair at not choosing, or willing, to be one's self; but that the deepest form of despair is to choose "to be another than himself." On the other hand "to will to be that self which one truly is, is indeed the opposite of despair," and this choice is the deepest responsibility of man. As I read some of his writings, I almost feel that he must have listened in on the statements made by our clients as they search and explore for the reality of self—often a painful and troubling search.

This exploration becomes even more disturbing when they find themselves involved in removing the false faces which they had not known were false faces. They begin to engage in the frightening task of exploring the turbulent and sometimes violent feelings within themselves. To remove a mask which you had thought was part of your real self can be a deeply disturbing experience, yet when there is freedom to think and feel and be, the individual moves toward such a goal. A few statements from a person who had completed a series of psychotherapeutic interviews, will illustrate this. She uses many metaphors as she tells how she struggled to get to the core of herself.

As I look at it now, I was peeling off layer after layer of defenses. I'd build them up, try them, and then discard them when you remained the same. I didn't know what was at the bottom and I was very much afraid to find out, but I had to keep on trying. At first, I felt there was nothing within me—just a great emptiness where I needed and wanted a solid core. Then I began to feel that I was facing a solid brick wall, too high to get over and too thick to go through. One day the wall became translucent, rather than solid. After this, the wall seemed to disappear, but beyond it I discovered a dam holding back violent, churning waters. I felt as if I were holding back the force of these waters and if I opened even a tiny hole, I and all about me would be destroyed in the ensuing torrent of feelings represented by the water. Finally I could stand the strain no longer and I let go. All I did, actually, was to succumb to complete and utter self-pity, then hate, then love. After this experience, I felt as if I had leaped a brink and was safely on the other side, though still tottering a bit on the edge. I don't know what I was searching for or where I was going, but I felt then, as I have always felt whenever I really lived, that I was moving forward.

I believe this represents rather well the feelings of many an individual that if the false front, the wall, the dam, is not maintained, then everything will be swept away in the violence of the feelings that he discovers pent-up in his private world. Yet it also illustrates the compelling necessity which the individual feels to search for and become himself. It also begins to indicate the way in which the individual determines the reality in himself—that when he fully experiences the feelings which at an organic level he is, as this client experienced her self-pity, hatred, and love, then he feels an assurance that he is being a part of his real self.

The Experiencing of Feeling

I would like to say something more about this experiencing of feeling. It is really the discovery of unknown elements of self. The phenomenon I am trying to describe is something which I think is quite difficult to get across in any meaningful way. In our daily lives there are a thousand and one reasons for not letting ourselves experience our attitudes fully, reasons from our past and from the present, reasons that reside within the social situation. It seems too dangerous, too potentially damaging, to experience them freely and fully. But in the safety and freedom of the therapeutic relationship, they can be experienced fully, clear to the limit of what they are. They can be and are experienced in a fashion that I like to think of as a "pure culture," so that for the moment the person is his fear, or he is his anger, or he is his tenderness, or whatever.

Perhaps again I can indicate that somewhat better by giving an example from a client that will indicate and convey something of what I mean. This comes from the recording of the thirty-first interview with this woman. She has talked several times of a recurrent feeling which troubles her and which she can't quite pin down and define. Is it a feeling that developed because she practically had no relationship with her parents? Is it a guilty feeling? She is not quite sure, and she ends this kind of talk with this statement:

Client: And I have the feeling that it isn't guilt. (Pause: she weeps) So . . . course I mean, I can't verbalize it yet. It's just being terribly hurt!

Therapist: M-hm. It isn't guilt except in the sense of being very much wounded somehow.

C: (Weeping) It's . . . you know, often I've been guilty of it myself, but in later years, when I've heard parents . . . say to their children, "stop crying," I've had a feeling, as though, well, why should they tell them to stop crying? They feel sorry for themselves, and who can feel more adequately sorry for himself than a child. Well, that is sort of what . . . I mean, as-as though I thought that they should let him cry. And . . . feel sorry for him too, maybe. In a . . . rather objective kind of way. Well, that's . . . that's something of the kind of thing I've been experiencing. I mean, now . . . just right now.

T: That catches a little more of the flavor of the feeling, that it's almost as if you're really weeping for yourself . . . .

C: And then of course, I've come to . . . to see and to feel that over this . . . see, I've covered it up. (Weeps) I've covered it up with so much bitterness, which in turn I've had to cover up. (Weeps) That's what I want to get rid of! I almost don't care if I hurt.

T: (Gently) You feel that here at the basis of it as you experienced it, is a feeling of real tears for yourself. But that you can't show, mustn't show, so that's been covered by bitterness that you don't like, that you'd like to be rid of. You almost feel you'd rather absorb the hurt than to . . . than to feel the bitterness. (Pause) And what you seem to be saying quite strongly is, I do hurt, and I've tried to cover it up.

C: I didn't know it.

T: M-hm. Like a new discovery really.

C: (Speaking at the same time) I never really did know. It's almost a physical thing. It's . . . it's sort of as though I were looking within myself at all kinds of . . . nerve endings and-and bits of-of . . . things that have been sort of mashed. (Weeping)

T: As though some of the most delicate aspects of you—physically almost — have been crushed or hurt.

C: Yes. And you know, I do get the feeling, oh, you poor thing. (Pause)

T: Just can't help but feel very deeply sorry for the person that is you.

I hope that perhaps this excerpt conveys a little bit of the thing I have been talking about, the experiencing of a feeling all the way to the limit. She was feeling herself as though she were nothing but hurt at that moment, nothing but sorrow for her crushed self. It is not only hurt and sorrow that are experienced in this all-out kind of fashion. It may be jealousy, or destructive anger, or deep desire, or confidence and pride, or sensitive tenderness, or shuddering fear, or outgoing love. It may be any of the emotions of which man is capable.

What I have gradually learned from experiences such as this is that the individual in such a moment is coming to be what he is. When a person has, throughout therapy, experienced in this fashion all the emotions which organismically arise in him, and has experienced them in this knowing and open manner, then he has experienced himself, in all the richness that exists within himself. He has become what he is.

The Discovery of Self in Experience

Let us pursue a bit further this question of what it means to become one's self. It is a most perplexing question and again I will try to take from a statement by a client, written between interviews, a suggestion of an answer. She tells how the various facades by which she has been living have somehow crumpled and collapsed, bringing a feeling of confusion, but also a feeling of relief. She continues:

You know, it seems as if all the energy that went into holding the arbitrary pattern together was quite unnecessary—a waste. You think you have to make the pattern yourself; but there are so many pieces, and it's so hard to see where they fit. Sometimes you put them in the wrong place, and the more pieces not fitted, the more effort it takes to hold them in place, until at last you are so tired that even that awful confusion is better than holding on any longer. Then you discover that left to themselves the jumbled pieces fall quite naturally into their own places, and a living pattern emerges without any effort at all on your part. Your job is just to discover it, and in the course of that, you will find yourself. You must even let your own experience tell you its own meaning; the minute you tell it what it means, you are at war with yourself.

Let me see if I can take her poetic expression and translate it into the meaning it has for me. I believe she is saying that to be herself means to find the pattern, the underlying order, which exists in the ceaselessly changing flow of her experience. Rather than to try to hold her experience into the form of a mask, or to make it be a form or structure that it is not, being herself means to discover the unity and harmony which exists in her own actual feelings and reactions. It means that the real self is something which is comfortably discovered in one's experience, not something imposed upon it.

Through giving excerpts from the statements of these clients, I have been trying to suggest what happens in the warmth and understanding of a facilitating relationship with a therapist. It seems that gradually, painfully, the individual explores what is behind the masks he presents to the world, and even behind the masks with which he has been deceiving himself. Deeply and often vividly he experiences the various elements of himself which have been hidden within. Thus to an increasing degree he becomes himself—not a facade of conformity to others, nor a cynical denial of all feeling, nor a front of intellectual rationality, but a living, breathing, feeling, fluctuating process—in short, he becomes a person.

The Person Who Emerges

I imagine that some of you are asking: "But what kind of a person does he become? It isn't enough to say that he drops the facades. What kind of person lies underneath?" Since one of the most obvious facts is that each individual tends to become a separate and distinct and unique person, the answer is not easy. However I would like to point out some of the characteristic trends which I see. No one person would fully exemplify these characteristics, no one person fully achieves the description I will give, but I do see certain generalizations which can be drawn, based upon living a therapeutic relationship with many clients.

Openness to Experience

First of all, I would say that in this process the individual becomes more open to his experience. This is a phrase which has come to have a great deal of meaning to me. It is the opposite of defensiveness. Psychological research has shown the way in which sensory evidence, if it runs contrary to the pattern of organization of the self, tends to be distorted in awareness. In other words we cannot see all that our senses report, but only the things which fit the picture we have.

Now in a safe relationship of the sort I have described, this defensiveness, or rigidity, tends to be replaced by an increasing openness to experience. The individual becomes more openly aware of his own feelings and attitudes as they exist in him at an organic level. He also becomes more aware of reality as it exists outside of himself, instead of perceiving it in preconceived categories. He sees that not all trees are green, not all men are stern fathers, not all women are rejecting, not all failure experiences prove that he is no good, and the like. He is able to take in the evidence in a new situation, as it is, rather than distorting it to fit a pattern which he already holds. As you might expect, this increasing ability to be open to experience makes him far more realistic in dealing with new people, new situations, new problems. It means that his beliefs are not rigid, that he can tolerate ambiguity. He can receive much conflicting evidence without forcing closure upon the situation. This openness of awareness to what exists at this moment in this situation is, I believe, an important element in the description of the person who emerges from therapy.

Perhaps I can give this concept a more vivid meaning if I illustrate it from a recorded interview. A young professional man reports in the forty-eighth interview the way in which he has become more open to some of his bodily sensations, as well as other feelings.

Client: It doesn't seem to me that it would be possible for anybody to relate all the changes that I feel. But I certainly have felt recently that I have more respect for, more objectivity toward, my physical makeup. I mean I don't expect too much of myself. This is how it works out. It feels to me that in the past I used to fight a certain tiredness that I felt after supper. Well, now I feel pretty sure that I really am tired—that I am not making myself tired— that I am just physiologically lower. It seemed that I was just constantly criticizing my tiredness.

Therapist: So you can let yourself be tired, instead of feeling along with it a kind of criticism of it.

C: Yes, that I shouldn't be tired or something. And it seems in a way to be pretty profound that I can just not fight this tiredness, and along with it goes a real feeling that being tired isn't such an awful thing. I think I can also kind of pick up a thread here of why I should be that way in the way my father is and the way he looks at some of these things. For instance, say that I was sick, and I would report this, and it would seem that overtly he would want to do something about it but he would also communicate, "Oh, my gosh, more trouble." You know, something like that.

T: As though there were something quite annoying really about being physically ill.

C: Yeah, I am sure that my father has the same disrespect for his own physiology that I have had. Now last summer I twisted my back, I wrenched it, I heard it snap and everything. There was real pain there all the time at first, real sharp. And I had the doctor look at it and he said it wasn't serious, it should heal by itself as long as I didn't bend too much. Well, this was months ago—and I have been noticing recently that—hell, this is real pain and it's still there—and it's not my fault.

T: It doesn't prove something bad about you—

C: No—and one of the reasons I seem to get more tired than I should maybe is because of this constant strain and so—I have already made an appointment with one of the doctors at the hospital that he would look at it and take an X-ray or something. In a way I guess you could say that I am just more accurately sensitive—or objectively sensitive to this kind of thing. I can say with certainty that this has also spread to what I eat and how much I eat. And this is really a profound change, and of course my relationship with my wife and the two children is—well, you just wouldn't recognize it if you could see me inside—as you have—I mean—there just doesn't seem to be anything more wonderful than really and genuinely—really feeling love for your own children and at the same time receiving it. I don't know how to put this. We have such an increased respect—both of us—for Judy and we've noticed just—as we participated in this—we have noticed such a tremendous change in her—it seems to be a pretty deep kind of thing.

T: It seems to me you are saying that you can listen more accurately to yourself. If your body says its tired, you listen to it and believe it, instead of criticizing it; if it's in pain, you can listen to that; if the feeling is really loving your wife or children, you can feel that, and it seems to show up in the differences in them too.

Here, in a relatively minor but symbolically important excerpt, can be seen much of what I have been trying to say about openness to experience. Formerly he could not freely feel pain or illness, because being ill meant being unacceptable. Neither could he feel tenderness and love for his child, because such feelings meant being weak, and he had to maintain his facade of being strong and masculine. But now he can be genuinely open to the experiences of his organism—he can be tired when he is tired, he can feel pain when his organism is in pain, he can freely experience the love he feels for his daughter, and he can also feel and express annoyance toward her, as he goes on to say in the next portion of the interview. He can fully live the experiences of his total organism, rather than shutting them out of awareness.

Trust in One's Organism

A second characteristic of the persons who emerge from therapy is that the person increasingly discovers that his own organism is trustworthy, that it is a suitable instrument for discovering the most satisfying behavior in each immediate situation.

If this seems strange, let me try to state it more fully. Perhaps it will help to understand my description if you think of the individual as faced with some existential choice: "Shall I go home to my family during vacation, or strike out on my own?" "Shall I drink this third cocktail which is being offered?" "Is this the person whom I would like to have as my partner in love and in life?" Thinking of such situations, what seems to be true of the person who emerges from the therapeutic process? To the extent that this person is open to all of his experience, he has access to all of the available data in the situation on which to base his behavior. He has knowledge of his own feelings and impulses, which are often complex and contradictory. He is freely able to sense the social demands, from the relatively rigid social "laws" to the desires of friends and family. He has access to his memories of similar situations, and the consequences of different behaviors in those situations. He has a relatively accurate perception of this existential situation in all of its complexity. He is better able to permit his total organism, his conscious thought participating, to consider, weigh, and balance each stimulus, need, and demand, and its relative weight and intensity. Out of this complex weighing and balancing he is able to discover that course of action which seems to come closest to satisfying all his needs in the situation, long-range as well as immediate needs.

In such a weighing and balancing of all of the components of a given life choice, his organism would not by any means be infallible. Mistaken choices might be made. But because he tends to be open to his experience, there is a greater and more immediate awareness of unsatisfying consequences, a quicker correction of choices which are in error.

It may help to realize that in most of us the defects which interfere with this weighing and balancing are that we include things which are not a part of our experience, and exclude elements which are. Thus an individual may persist in the concept that "I can handle liquor," when openness to his past experience would indicate that this is scarcely correct. Or a young woman may see only the good qualities of her prospective mate, where an openness to experience would indicate that he possesses faults as well.

In general, then, it appears to be true that when a client is open to his experience, he comes to find his organism more trustworthy. He feels less fear of the emotional reactions which he has. There is a gradual growth of trust in, and even affection for, the complex, rich, varied assortment of feelings and tendencies which exist in him at the organic level. Consciousness, instead of being the watchman over a dangerous and unpredictable lot of impulses, of which few can be permitted to see the light of day, becomes the comfortable inhabitant of a society of impulses and feelings and thoughts, which are discovered to be very satisfactorily self-governing when not fearfully guarded.

An Internal Locus of Evaluation

Another trend which is evident in this process of becoming a person relates to the source or locus of choices and decisions, of evaluative judgments. The individual increasingly comes to feel that this locus of evaluation lies within himself. Less and less does he look to others for approval or disapproval; for standards to live by; for decisions and choices. He recognizes that it rests within himself to choose; that the only question which matters is: "Am I living in a way which is deeply satisfying to me, and which truly expresses me?" This I think is perhaps the most important question for the creative individual.

Perhaps it will help if I give an illustration. I would like to give a brief portion of a recorded interview with a young woman, a graduate student, who had come for counseling help. She was initially very much disturbed about many problems, and had been contemplating suicide. During the interviews one of the feelings she discovered was her great desire to be dependent, just to let someone else take over the direction of her life. She was very critical of those who had not given her enough guidance. She talked about one after another of her professors, feeling bitterly that none of them had taught her anything with deep meaning. Gradually she began to realize that part of the difficulty was the fact that she had taken no initiative in participating in these classes. Then comes the portion I wish to quote.

I think you will find that this excerpt gives you some indication of what it means in experience to accept the locus of evaluation as being within oneself. Here then is the quotation from one of the later interviews with this young woman as she has begun to realize that perhaps she is partly responsible for the deficiencies in her own education.

Client: Well now, I wonder if I've been going around doing that, getting smatterings of things, and not getting hold, not really getting down to things.

Therapist: Maybe you've been getting just spoonfuls here and there rather than really digging in somewhere rather deeply.

C: M-hm. That's why I say—(slowly and very thoughtfully) well, with that sort of a foundation, well, it's really up to me. I mean, it seems to be really apparent to me that I can't depend on someone else to give me an education. (very softly) I'll really have to get it myself.

T: It really begins to come home—there's only one person that can educate you—a realization that perhaps nobody else can give you an education.

C: M-hm. (long pause—while she sits thinking) I have all the symptoms of fright (laughs softly).

T: Fright? That this is a scary thing, is that what you mean?

C: M-hm. (very long pause—obviously struggling with feelings in herself).

T: Do you want to say any more about what you mean by that? That it really does give you the symptoms of fright?

C: (laughs) I, uh—I don't know whether I quite know. I mean—well, it really seems like I'm cut loose (pause), and it seems that I'm very—I don't know—in a vulnerable position, but I, uh, I brought this up and it, uh, somehow it almost came out without my saying it. It seems to be—it's something I let out.

T: Hardly a part of you.

C: Well, I felt surprised.

T: As though: "Well for goodness sake, did I say that?" (both chuckle).

C: Really, I don't think I've had that feeling before. I've—uh, well, this really feels like I'm saying something that, uh, is a part of me really. (pause) Or, uh, (quite perplexed) it feels like I sort of have, uh, I don't know. I have a feeling of strength, and yet, I have a feeling of—realizing it's so sort of fearful, of fright.

T: That is, do you mean that saying something of that sort gives you at the same time a feeling of, of strength in saying it, and yet at the same time a frightened feeling of what you have said, is that it?

C: M-hm. I am feeling that. For instance, I'm feeling it internally now—a sort of surging up, or force. As if that's something really big and strong. And yet, uh, well at first it was almost a physical feeling of just being out alone, and sort of cut off from a—support I had been carrying around.

T: You feel that it's something deep and strong, and surging forth, and at the same time, you just feel as though you'd cut yourself loose from any support when you say it.

C: M-hm. Maybe that's—I don't know—it's a disturbance of a kind of pattern I've been carrying around, I think.

T: It sort of shakes a rather significant pattern, jars it loose.

C: M-hm. (pause, then cautiously, but with conviction) I, I think—I don't know, but I have the feeling that then I am going to begin to do more things that I know I should do. . . . There are so many things that I need to do. It seems in so many avenues of my living I have to work out new ways of behaving, but—maybe—I can see myself doing a little better in some things.

I hope that this illustration gives some sense of the strength which is experienced in being a unique person, responsible for oneself, and also the uneasiness that accompanies this assumption of responsibility.

Willingness to be a Process

I should like to point out one final characteristic of these individuals as they strive to discover and become themselves. It is that the individual seems to become more content to be a process than a product. When he enters the therapeutic relationship, the client is likely to wish to achieve some fixed state; he wants to reach the point where his problems are solved, or where he is effective in his work, or where his marriage is satisfactory. He tends, in the freedom of the therapeutic relationship, to drop such fixed goals, and to accept a more satisfying realization that he is not a fixed entity, but a process of becoming.

One client, at the conclusion of therapy, says in rather puzzled fashion: "I haven't finished the job of integrating and reorganizing myself, but that's only confusing, not discouraging, now that I realize this is a continuing process. . . . It is exciting, sometimes upsetting, but deeply encouraging to feel yourself in action, apparently knowing where you are going even though you don't always consciously know what that is." One can see here both the expression of trust in the organism, which I have mentioned, and also the realization of self as a process.

Here is another statement of this same element of fluidity of existential living. "This whole train of experiencing, and the meanings that I have thus far discovered in it, seem to have launched me on a process which is both fascinating and at times a little frightening. It seems to mean letting my experience carry me on, in a direction which appears to be forward, toward goals that I can but dimly define, as I try to understand at least the current meaning of that experience. The sensation is that of floating with a complex stream of experience, with the fascinating possibility of trying to comprehend its ever-changing complexity." Here again is a personal description of what it seems like to accept oneself as a stream of becoming, not a finished product. It means that a person is a fluid process, not a fixed and static entity; a flowing river of change, not a block of solid material; a continually changing constellation of potentialities, not a fixed quantity of traits.

Conclusion

I have tried to tell you what has seemed to occur in the lives of people with whom I have had the privilege of being in a relationship as they struggled toward becoming themselves. I have endeavored to describe, as accurately as I can, the meanings which seem to be involved in this process of becoming a person. I am sure that I do not see it clearly or completely, since I keep changing in my comprehension and understanding of it. I hope you will accept it as a current and tentative picture, not as something final.

One reason for stressing the tentative nature of what I have said is that I wish to make it clear that I am not saying: "This is what you should become; here is the goal for you." Rather, I am saying that these are some of the meanings I see in the experiences that my clients and I have shared. Perhaps this picture of the experience of others may illuminate or give more meaning to some of your own experiences.

I have pointed out that the individual appears to have a strong desire to become himself; that given a favorable psychological climate he drops the defensive masks with which he has faced life, and begins to discover and to experience the stranger who lives behind these masks—the hidden parts of himself. I have pictured some of the attributes of the person who emerges—the tendency to be more open to all elements of his organic experience; the growth of trust in one's organism as an instrument of sensitive living; the acceptance of the fearsome responsibility of being a unique person; and finally the sense of living in one's life as a participant in a fluid, ongoing process, continually discovering new aspects of one's self in the flow of experience. These are some of the things which seem to me to be involved in becoming a person.

SIGNIFICANT ASPECTS OF
CLIENT-CENTERED THERAPY

IN planning to address this group, I have considered and discarded several possible topics. I was tempted to describe the process of non-directive therapy and the counselor techniques and procedures which seem most useful in bringing about this process. But much of this material is now in writing. My own book on counseling and psychotherapy contains much of the basic material, and my recent more popular book on counseling with returning servicemen tends to supplement it. The philosophy of the client-centered approach and its application to work with children is persuasively presented by Allen. The application to counseling of industrial employees is discussed in the volume by Cantor. Curran has now published in book form one of the several research studies which are throwing new light on both process and procedure. Axline is publishing a book on play and group therapy. Snyder is bringing out a book of cases. So it seems unnecessary to come a long distance to summarize material which is, or soon will be obtainable in written form.

Another tempting possibility, particularly in this setting, was to discuss some of the roots from which the client-centered approach has sprung. It would have been interesting to show how in its concepts of repression and release, in its stress upon catharsis and insight, it has many roots in Freudian thinking, and to acknowledge that indebtedness. Such an analysis could also have shown that in its concept of the individual's ability to organize his own experience there is an even deeper indebtedness to the work of Rank, Taft, and Allen. In its stress upon objective research, the subjecting of fluid attitudes to scientific investigation, the willingness to submit all hypotheses to a verification or disproof by research methods, the debt is obviously to the whole field of American psychology, with its genius for scientific methodology. It could also have been pointed out that although everyone in the clinical field has been heavily exposed to the eclectic "team" approach to therapy of the child guidance movement, and the somewhat similar eclecticism of the Adolf Meyers – Hopkins school of thought, these eclectic viewpoint have perhaps not been so fruitful in therapy and that little from these sources has been retained in the nondirective approach. It might also have been pointed out that in its basic trend away from guiding and directing the client, the non-directive approach is deeply rooted in practical clinical experience, and is in accord with the experience of most clinical workers, so much so that one of the commonest reactions of experienced therapists is that "You have crystallized and put into words something that I have been groping toward in my own experience for a long time."

Such an analysis, such a tracing of root ideas, needs to be made, but I doubt my own ability to make it. I am also doubtful that anyone who is deeply concerned with a new development knows with any degree of accuracy where his ideas came from.

Consequently I am, in this presentation. Adopting a third pathway. While I shall bring in a brief description of process and procedure, and while I shall acknowledge in a general way our indebtedness to many root sources, and shall recognize the many common elements shared by client-centered therapy and other approaches, I believe it will be to our mutual advantage if I stress primarily those aspects in which nondirective therapy differs most sharply and deeply from other therapeutic procedures. I hope to point out some of the basically significant ways in which the client-centered viewpoint differs from others, not only in its present principles, but in the wider divergencies which are implied by the projection of its central principles.

THE PREDICTABLE PROCESS OF CLIENT-CENTERED THERAPY

The first of the three distinctive elements of client-centered therapy to which I wish to call your attention is the predictability of the therapeutic process in this approach. We find, both clinically and statistically, that a predictable pattern of therapeutic development takes place. The assurance which we feel about this was brought home to me recently when I played a recorded first interview for the graduate students in our practicum immediately after it was recorded, pointing out the characteristic aspects, and agreeing to play later interviews for them to let them see the later phases of the counseling process. The fact that I knew with assurance what the later pattern would be before it had occurred only struck me as I thought about the incident. We have become clinically so accustomed to this predictable quality that we take it for granted. Perhaps a brief summarized description of this therapeutic process will indicate those elements of which we feel sure.

It may be said that we now know how to initiate a complex and predictable chain of events in dealing with the maladjusted individual, a chain of events which is therapeutic, and which operates effectively in problem situations of the most diverse type. This predictable chain of events may come about through the use of language as in counseling, through symbolic language, as in play therapy, through disguised language as in drama or puppet therapy. It is effective in dealing with individual situations, and also in small group situations.

It is possible to state with some exactness the conditions which must be met in order to initiate and carry through this releasing therapeutic experience. Below are listed in brief form the conditions which seem to be necessary, and the therapeutic results which occur.

This experience which releases the growth forces within the individual will come about in most cases if the following elements are present.

1. If the counselor operates on the principle that the individual is basically responsible for himself, and is willing for the individual to keep that responsibility.

2. If the counselor operates on the principle that the client has a strong drive to become mature, socially adjusted, independent, productive, and relies on this force, not on his own powers, for therapeutic change.

3. If the counselor creates a warm and permissive atmosphere in which the individual is free to bring out any attitudes and feelings which he may have, no matter how unconventional, absurd, or contradictory these attitudes may be. The client is as free to withhold expression as he is to give expression to his feelings.

4. If the limits which are set are simple limits set on behavior, and not limits set on attitudes. (This applies mostly to children. The child may not be permitted to break a window or leave the room, but he is free to feel like breaking a window, and the feeling is fully accepted. The adult client may not be permitted more than an hour for an interview, but there is full acceptance of his desire to claim more time.)

5. If the therapist uses only those procedures and techniques in the interview which convey his deep understanding of the emotionalized attitudes expressed and his acceptance of them. This understanding is perhaps best conveyed by a sensitive reflection and clarification of the client's attitudes. The counselor's acceptance involves neither approval nor disapproval.

6. If the counselor refrains from any expression or action which is contrary to the preceding principles. This means refraining from questioning, probing, blame, interpretation, advice, suggestion, persuasion, reassurance.

If these conditions are met, then it may be said with assurance that in the great majority of cases the following results will take place.

1. The client will express deep and motivating attitudes.

2. The client will explore his own attitudes and reactions more fully than he has previously done and will come to be aware of aspects of his attitudes which he has previously denied.

3. He will arrive at a clearer conscious realization of his motivating attitudes and will accept himself more completely. This realization and this acceptance will include attitudes previously denied. He may or may not verbalize this clearer conscious understanding of himself and his behavior.

4. In the light of his clearer perception of himself he will choose, on his own initiative and on his own responsibility, new goals which are more satisfying than his maladjusted goals.

5. He will choose to behave in a different fashion in order to reach these goals, and this new behavior will be in the direction of greater psychological growth and maturity. It will also be more spontaneous and less tense, more in harmony with social needs of others, will represent a more realistic and more comfortable adjustment to life. It will be more integrated than his former behavior. It will be a step forward in the life of the individual.

The best scientific description of this process is that supplied by Snyder. Analyzing a number of cases with strictly objective research techniques, Snyder has discovered that the development in these cases is roughly parallel, that the initial phase of catharsis is replaced by a phase in which insight becomes the most significant element, and this in turn by a phase marked by the increase in positive choice and action.

Clinically, we know that sometimes this process is relatively shallow, involving primarily a fresh reorientation to an immediate problem, and in other instances so deep as to involve a complete reorientation of personality. It is recognizably the same process whether it involves a girl who is unhappy in a dormitory and is able in three interviews to see something of her childishness and dependence, and to take steps in a mature direction, or whether it involves a young man who is on the edge of a schizophrenic break, and who in thirty interviews works out deep insights in relation to his desire for his father's death, and his possessive and incestuous impulses toward his mother, and who not only takes new steps but rebuilds his whole personality in the process. Whether shallow or deep, it is basically the same.

We are coming to recognize with assurance characteristic aspects of each phase of the process. We know that the catharsis involves a gradual and more complete expression of emotionalized attitudes. We know that characteristically the conversation goes from superficial problems and attitudes to deeper problems and attitudes. We know that this process of exploration gradually unearths relevant attitudes which have been denied to consciousness. We recognize too that the process of achieving insight is likely to involve more adequate facing of reality as it exists within the self, as well as external reality; that it involves the relating of problems to each other, the perception of patterns of behavior; that it involves the acceptance of hitherto denied elements of the self, and a reformulating of the self-concept; and that it involves the making of new plans.

In the final phase we know that the choice of new ways of behaving will be in conformity with the newly organized concept of the self; that first steps in putting these plans into action will be small but symbolic; that the individual will feel only a minimum degree of confidence that he can put his plans into effect, that later steps implement more and more completely the new concept of self, and that this process continues beyond the conclusion of the therapeutic interviews.

If these statements seem to contain too much assurance, to sound "too good to be true," I can only say that for many of them we now have research backing, and that as rapidly as possible we are developing our research to bring all phases of the process under objective scrutiny. Those of us working clinically with client-centered therapy regard this predictability as a settled characteristic, even though we recognize that additional research will be necessary to fill out the picture more completely.

It is the implication of this predictability which is startling. Whenever, in science, a predictable process has been discovered, it has been found possible to use it as a starting point for a whole chain of discoveries. We regard this as not only entirely possible, but inevitable, with regard to this predictable process in therapy. Hence, we regard this orderly and predictable nature of nondirective therapy as one of its most distinctive and significant points of difference from other approaches. Its importance lies not only in the fact that it is a present difference, but in the fact that it points toward a sharply different future, in which scientific exploration of this known chain of events should lead to many new discoveries, developments, and applications.

THE DISCOVERY OF THE CAPACITY OF THE CLIENT

Naturally the question is raised, what is the reason for this predictability in a type of therapeutic procedure in which the therapist serves
only a catalytic function? Basically the reason for the predictability
of the therapeutic process lies in the discovery—and I use that word
intentionally—that within the client reside constructive forces whose
strength and uniformity have been either entirely unrecognized or
grossly underestimated. It is the clear-cut and disciplined reliance by
the therapist upon those forces within the client, which seems to account for the orderliness of the therapeutic process, and its consistency
from one client to the next.

I mentioned that I regarded this as a discovery. I would like to amplify
that statement. We have known for centuries that catharsis and emotional release were helpful. Many new methods have been and are being
developed to bring about release, but the principle is not new. Likewise,
we have known since Freud's time that insight, if it is accepted and assimilated by the client, is therapeutic. The principle is not new. Likewise,
we have realized that revised action patterns, new ways of behaving, may
come about as a result of insight. The principle is not new.

But we have not known or recognized that in most if not all individuals there exist growth forces, tendencies toward self-actualization,
which may act as the sole motivation for therapy. We have not realized
that under suitable psychological conditions these forces bring about
emotional release in those areas and at those rates which are most ben-
eficial to the individual. These forces drive the individual to explore
his own attitudes and his relationship to reality, and to explore these
areas effectively. We have not realized that the individual is capable
of exploring his attitudes and feelings, including those which have
been denied to consciousness, at a rate which does not cause panic, and
to the depth required for comfortable adjustment. The individual is
capable of discovering and perceiving, truly and spontaneously, the
interrelationships between his own attitudes, and the relationship of
himself to reality. The individual has the capacity and the strength to
devise, quite unguided, the steps which will lead him to a more mature
and more comfortable relationship to his reality. It is the gradual and
increasing recognition of these capacities within the individual by the
client-centered therapist that rates, I believe, the term discovery. All
of these capacities I have described are released in the individual if a
suitable psychological atmosphere is provided.

There has, of course, been lip service paid to the strength of the
client, and the need of utilizing the urge toward independence which

exists in the client. Psychiatrists, analysts, and especially social case workers have stressed this point. Yet it is clear from what is said, and even more clear from the case material cited, that this confidence is a very limited confidence. It is a confidence that the client can take over, if guided by the expert, a confidence that the client can assimilate insight if it is first given to him by the expert, can make choices providing guidance is given at crucial points. It is, in short, the same sort of attitude which the mother has toward the adolescent, that she believes in his capacity to make his own decisions and guide his own life, providing he takes the directions of which she approves.

This is very evident in the latest book on psychoanalysis by Alexander and French. Although many of the former views and practices of psychoanalysis are discarded, and the procedures are far more nearly in line with those of nondirective therapy, it is still the therapist who is definitely in control. He gives the insights, he is ready to guide at crucial points. Thus while the authors state that the aim of the therapist is to free the patient to develop his capacities, and to increase his ability to satisfy his needs in ways acceptable to himself and society; and while they speak of the basic conflict between competition and cooperation as one which the individual must settle for himself; and speak of the integration of new insight as a normal function of the ego, it is clear when they speak of procedures that they have no confidence that the client has the capacity to do any of these things. For in practice, "As soon as the therapist takes the more active role we advocate, systematic planning becomes imperative. In addition to the original decision as to the particular sort of strategy to be employed in the treatment of any case, we recommend the conscious use of various techniques in a flexible manner, shifting tactics to fit the particular needs of the moment. Among these modifications of the standard technique are; using not only the method of free association but interviews of a more direct character, manipulating the frequency of the interviews, giving directives to the patient concerning his daily life, employing interruptions of long or short duration in preparation for ending the treatment, regulating the transference relationship to meet the specific needs of the case, and making use of real-life experiences as an integral part of therapy." At least this leaves no doubt as to whether it is the client's or the therapist's hour; it is clearly the latter. The capacities which the client is to develop are clearly not to be developed in the therapeutic sessions.

The client-centered therapist stands at an opposite pole, both theoretically and practically. He has learned that the constructive forces in the individual can be trusted, and that the more deeply they are relied upon, the more deeply they are released. He has come to build his procedures upon these hypotheses, which are rapidly becoming established as facts; that the client knows the areas of concern which he is ready to explore; that the client is the best judge as to the most desirable frequency of interviews; that the client can lead the way more efficiently than the therapist into deeper concerns; that the client will protect himself from panic by ceasing to explore an area which is becoming too painful; that the client can and will uncover all the repressed elements which it is necessary to uncover in order to build a comfortable adjustment; that the client can achieve for himself far truer and more sensitive and accurate insights than can possibly be given to him; that the client is capable of translating these insights into constructive behavior which weigh his own needs and desires realistically against the demands of society; that the client knows when therapy is completed and he is ready to cope with life independently. Only one condition is necessary for all these forces to be released, and that is the proper psychological atmosphere between client and therapist.

Our case records and increasingly our research bear out these statements. One might suppose that there would be a generally favorable reaction to this discovery, since it amounts in effect to tapping great reservoirs of hitherto little-used energy. Quite the contrary is true, however, in professional groups. There is no other aspect of client-centered therapy which comes under such vigorous attack. It seems to be genuinely disturbing to many professional people to entertain the thought that this client upon whom they have been exercising their professional skill actually knows more about his inner psychological self than they can possibly know, and that he possesses constructive strengths which make the constructive push by the therapist seem puny indeed by comparison. The willingness fully to accept this strength of the client, with all the re-orientation of therapeutic procedure which it implies, is one of the ways in which client-centered therapy differs most sharply from other therapeutic approaches.

THE CLIENT-CENTERED NATURE OF THE THERAPEUTIC RELATIONSHIP

The third distinctive feature of this type of therapy is the character of the relationship between therapist and client. Unlike other therapies in which the skills of the therapist are to be exercised upon the client, in this approach the skills of the therapist are focused upon creating a psychological atmosphere in which the client can work. If the counselor can create a relationship permeated by warmth, understanding, safety from any type of attack, no matter how trivial, and basic acceptance of the person as he is, then the client will drop his natural defensiveness and use the situation. As we have puzzled over the characteristics of a successful therapeutic relationship, we have come to feel that the sense of communication is very important. If the client feels that he is actually communicating his present attitudes, superficial, confused, or conflicted as they may be, and that his communication is understood rather than evaluated in any way, then he is freed to communicate more deeply. A relationship in which the client thus feels that he is communicating is almost certain to be fruitful.

All of this means a drastic reorganization in the counselor's thinking, particularly if he has previously utilized other approaches. He gradually learns that the statement that the time is to be "the client's hour" means just that, and that his biggest task is to make it more and more deeply true.

Perhaps something of the characteristics of the relationship may be suggested by excerpts from a paper written by a young minister who has spent several months learning client-centered counseling procedures.

"Because the client-centered, nondirective counseling approach has been rather carefully defined and clearly illustrated, it gives the "Illusion of Simplicity." The technique seems deceptively easy to master. Then you begin to practice. A word is wrong here and there. You don't quite reflect feeling, but reflect content instead. It is difficult to handle questions; you are tempted to interpret. Nothing seems so serious that further practice won't correct it. Perhaps you are having trouble playing two roles—that of minister and that of counselor. Bring up the question in class and the matter is solved again with a deceptive ease. But these apparently minor errors and a certain woodenness of response seem exceedingly persistent.

"Only gradually does it dawn that if the technique is true it demands a feeling of warmth. You begin to feel that the attitude is the thing. Every little word is not so important if you have the correct accepting and permissive attitude toward the client. So you bear down on the permissiveness and acceptance. You will permiss and accept and reflect the client, if it kills you!

"But you still have those troublesome questions from the client. He simply doesn't know the next step. He asks you to give him a hint, some possibilities, after all you are expected to know something, else why is he here! As a minister, you ought to have some convictions about what people should believe, how they should act. As a counselor, you should know something about removing this obstacle—you ought to have the equivalent of the surgeon's knife and use it. Then you begin to wonder. The technique is good, but . . . does it go far enough! does it really work on clients? is it right to leave a person helpless, when you might show him the way out?

"Here it seems to me is the crucial point. "Narrow is the gate" and hard the path from here on. So one else can give satisfying answers and even the instructors seem frustrating because they appear not to be helpful in your specific case. For here is demanded of you what no other person can do or point out—and that is to rigorously scrutinize yourself and your attitudes towards others. Do you believe that all people truly have a creative potential in them? That each person is a unique individual and that he alone can work out his own individuality? Or do you really believe that some persons are of "negative value" and others are weak and must be led and taught by "wiser," "stronger" people.

"You begin to see that there is nothing compartmentalized about this method of counseling. It is not just counseling, because it demands the most exhaustive, penetrating, and comprehensive consistency. In other methods you can shape tools, pick them up for use when you will. But when genuine acceptance and permissiveness are your tools it requires nothing less than the whole complete personality. And to grow oneself is the most demanding of all."

He goes on to discuss the notion that the counselor must be restrained and "self-denying." He concludes that this is a mistaken notion.

"Instead of demanding less of the counselor's personality in the situation, client-centered counseling in some ways demands more. It demands discipline, not restraint. It calls for the utmost in sensitivity, appreciative awareness, channeled and disciplined. It demands that the counselor put all he has of these precious qualities into the situation, but in a disciplined, refined manner. It is restraint only in the sense that the counselor does not express himself in certain areas that he may use himself in others.

"Even this is deceptive, however. It is not so much restraint in any area as it is a focusing, sensitizing one's energies and personality in the direction of an appreciative and understanding attitude."

As time has gone by we have come to put increasing stress upon the "client-centeredness" of the relationship, because it is more effective the more completely the counselor concentrates upon trying to understand the client as the client seems to himself. As I look back upon some of our earlier published cases—the case of Herbert Bryan in my book, or Snyder's case of Mr. M.—I realize that we have gradually dropped the vestiges of subtle directiveness which are all too evident in those cases. We have come to recognize that if we can provide understanding of the way the client seems to himself at this moment, he can do the rest. The therapist must lay aside his preoccupation with diagnosis and his diagnostic shrewdness, must discard his tendency to make professional evaluations, must cease his endeavors to formulate an accurate prognosis, must give up the temptation subtly to guide the individual, and must concentrate on one purpose only; that of providing deep understanding and acceptance of the attitudes consciously held at this moment by the client as he explores step by step into the dangerous areas which he has been denying to consciousness.

I trust it is evident from this description that this type of relationship can exist only if the counselor is deeply and genuinely able to adopt these attitudes. Client-centered counseling, if it is to be effective, cannot be a trick or a tool. It is not a subtle way of guiding the client while pretending to let him guide himself. To be effective, it must be genuine. It is this sensitive and sincere "client-centeredness" in the therapeutic relationship that I regard as the third characteristic of nondirective therapy which sets it distinctively apart from other approaches.

SOME IMPLICATIONS

Although the client-centered approach had its origin purely within the limits of the psychological clinic, it is proving to have implications, often of a startling nature, for very diverse fields of effort. I should like to suggest a few of these present and potential implications.

In the field of psychotherapy itself, it leads to conclusions that seem distinctly heretical. It appears evident that training and practice in therapy should probably precede training in the field of diagnosis. Diagnostic knowledge and skill is not necessary for good therapy, a statement which sounds like blasphemy to many, and if the professional worker, whether psychiatrist, psychologist or caseworker, received training in therapy first he would learn psychological dynamics in a truly dynamic fashion, and would acquire a professional humility and willingness to learn from his client which is today all too rare.

The viewpoint appears to have implications for medicine. It has fascinated me to observe that when a prominent allergist began to use client-centered therapy for the treatment of non-specific allergies, he found not only very good therapeutic results, but the experience began to affect his whole medical practice. It has gradually meant the reorganization of his office procedure. He has given his nurses a new type of training in understanding the patient. He has decided to have all medical histories taken by a nonmedical person trained in nondirective techniques, in order to get a true picture of the client's feelings and attitudes toward himself and his health, uncluttered by the bias and diagnostic evaluation which is almost inevitable when a medical person

takes the history and unintentionally distorts the material by his premature judgments. He has found these histories much more helpful to
the physicians than those taken by physicians.

The client-centered viewpoint has already been shown to have significant implications for the field of survey interviewing and public
opinion study. Use of such techniques by Likert, Lazarsfeld, and others
has meant the elimination of much of the factor of bias in such studies.

This approach has also, we believe, deep implications for the handling of social and group conflicts, as I have pointed out in another paper. Our work in applying a client-centered viewpoint to group therapy
situations, while still in its early stages, leads us to feel that a significant clue to the constructive solution of interpersonal and intercultural
frictions in the group may be in our hands. Application of these procedures to staff groups, to inter-racial groups, to groups with personal
problems and tensions, is under way.

In the field of education, too, the client-centered approach is finding
significant application. The work of Cantor, a description of which will
soon be published, is outstanding in this connection, but a number of
teachers are finding that these methods, designed for therapy, produce
a new type of educational process, an independent learning which is
highly desirable, and even a reorientation of individual direction which
is very similar to the results of individual or group therapy.

Even in the realm of our philosophical orientation, the client-centered approach has its deep implications. I should like to indicate this
by quoting briefly from a previous paper.

As we examine and try to evaluate our clinical experience with client-centered therapy, the phenomenon of the reorganization of attitudes and the redirection of behavior by the individual assumes greater
and greater importance. This phenomenon seems to find inadequate
explanation in terms of the determinism which is the predominant
philosophical background of most psychological work. The capacity
of the individual to reorganize his attitudes and behavior in ways not
determined by external factors nor by previous elements in his own
experience, but determined by his own insight into those factors, is an
impressive capacity. It involves a basic spontaneity which we have been
loathe to admit into our scientific thinking.

The clinical experience could be summarized by saying that the behavior of the human organism may be determined by the influences to
which it has been exposed, but it may also be determined by the creative
and integrative insight of the organism itself. This ability of the person
to discover new meaning in the forces which impinge upon him and in
the past experiences which have been controlling him, and the ability

to alter consciously his behavior in the light of this new meaning, has a profound significance for our thinking which has not been fully realized. We need to revise the philosophical basis of our work to a point where it can admit that forces exist within the individual which can exercise a spontaneous and significant influence upon behavior which is not predictable through knowledge of prior influences and conditionings. The forces released through a catalytic process of therapy are not adequately accounted for by a knowledge of the individual's previous conditionings, but only if we grant the presence of a spontaneous force within the organism which has the capacity of integration and redirection. This capacity for volitional control is a force which we must take into account in any psychological equation.

So we find an approach which began merely as a way of dealing with problems of human maladjustment forcing us into a revaluation of our basic philosophical concepts.

SUMMARY

I hope that throughout this paper I have managed to convey what is my own conviction, that what we now know or think we know about a client-centered approach is only a beginning, only the opening of a door beyond which we are beginning to see some very challenging roads, some fields rich with opportunity. It is the facts of our clinical and research experience which keep pointing forward into new and exciting possibilities. Yet whatever the future may hold, it appears already clear that we are dealing with materials of a new and significant nature, which demand the most openminded and thorough exploration. If our present formulations of those facts are correct, then we would say that some important elements already stand out; that certain basic attitudes and skills can create a psychological atmosphere which releases, frees, and utilizes deep strengths in the client; that these strengths and capacities are more sensitive and more rugged than hitherto supposed; and that they are released in an orderly and predictable process which may prove as significant a basic fact in social science as some of the laws and predictable processes in the physical sciences.

SELECTED REFERENCES

1.   ALEXANDER, F. AND FRENCH, T. Psychoanalytic Therapy. New York: Ronald Press, 1946.

2. ALLEN, F. Psychotherapy with Children. New York: Norton, 1942.
3. CANTOR, N. Employee Counseling. New York: McGraw-Hill Book Company.
4. CANTOR, N. The Dynamics of Learning. (unpublished mss.) University of Buffalo, 1943.
5. CURRAN, C. A. Personality Factors in Counseling. New York: Grune and Stratton, 1945.
6. RANK, O. Will Therapy. New York: Alfred A. Knopf 1936.
7. ROGERS, C. R. "Counseling", Review of Educational Research. April 1945 (Vol. 15), pp. 135-163.
8. ROGERS, C. R. Counseling and Psychotherapy. New York: Houghton Mifflin Co., 1942.
9. ROGERS, C. R. The implications of nondirective therapy for the handling of social conflicts. Paper given to a seminar of the Bureau of Intercultural Education, New York City, Feb. 18, 1946.
10. ROGERS. C. R. AND WALLEN, J. L. Counseling with Returned Servicemen. New York: McGraw-Hill, 1946.
11. SNYDER, W. U. "An Investigation of the Nature of Non-Directive Psychotherapy." Journal of General Psychology. Vol. 33, 1945. pp.193-223.
12. TAFT, J. The Dynamics of Therapy in a Controlled Relationship. New York: Macmillan, 1933.

THE PROCESSES OF THERAPY

Recent years have brought significant progress in the field of psychotherapy. The help obtained by the individual in a series of treatment interviews is no longer a vague mystery impossible of serious investigation. Social workers, psychiatrists, and clinical psychologists working in this field have developed an increased understanding of the therapeutic process, and a greater degree of assurance in its use. The time is perhaps ripe for various workers to endeavor to formulate and describe the fundamental aspects of this process, in order that such descriptions may serve as hypotheses to be tested by research. This paper is an attempt to present such an analysis of the process of therapy. The ideas expressed are drawn from many sources, particularly from those with actual experience in treatment work.

Before a person can receive help from a therapist or counselor, it is essential that certain basic conditions be met. It is probably necessary that the client, whether child or adult, should feel some dissatisfaction with present adjustment, some fundamental need of help. Other treatment techniques, such as changes in the environment, may be effective without this feeling of need, but therapy, as the word has come to be used, can scarcely take place without it. Likewise, therapy has no chance of being successful if there is too heavy a weight of adverse social factors making adjustment impossible except through radical alteration of circumstances. It is also necessary that the client have intelligence above the borderline level. These would seem to be the essential conditions for therapy. Research upon each of these points would be most helpful in determining the range of situations in which psychotherapy may be effective.

Granted these conditions, and a skilled therapist whose purpose is to release and strengthen the individual, rather than to intervene in his life, certain processes seem to take place, or if they do not take place, therapy is likely to be unsuccessful. These processes are described below. It should be noted that there is overlapping between these steps, and they do not always occur in the order in which they are set forth. The experiences described might be differently formulated or placed in different categories by some other therapist. Yet in most successful therapeutic experiences, where the individual leaves the contacts more able to handle his own problems, it is the writer's opinion that each of these steps will have been fulfilled.

I.   Rapport is established:

There must be a warmth of relationship between counselor and counselee if any progress is to be made. Interviewing "tricks" will not do. There must be on the part of the counselor a genuine interest in the individual, a degree of identification which is none the less real because it is understood and to some extent controlled. Identification and objectivity are delicately balanced components in the counselor's approach.

In successful therapy these attitudes on the part of the therapist help to build up in the client the confidence and trust which make possible the subsequent elements in the process. The rapport which is established is a lasting thing throughout therapy, and constitutes a personal bond which needs to be gradually broken at the conclusion of the interviews. While its emotional value for the client is much greater than for the therapist, yet both are involved and do much better to admit this involvement frankly.

II.   There is free expression of feeling on the part of the client:

Some of our most significant recent advances in therapy have been in this area. The values of catharsis, of release of feeling, have long been recognized, but only recently have we learned new ways of encouraging such release. The development of play therapy which uses all sorts of media for expression, and the development of psychodramatics are indications that we have only begun to discover the possible procedures in this field. In interview techniques progress has also been made so that we tend to avoid that blocking of free expression which is so characteristic of our older case records. It is worth noting that some schools of thought encourage expression of material related to past experience, others material related to present feelings. There seems to be no evidence that one is more therapeutic than the other, since, in an important sense, "all roads lead to Rome." Our most profound emotional patterns are as evident in our daily experience as in our past history, as plain in the immediate counseling relationship as in our childhood reactions.

III. Recognition and acceptance, by the client, of his spontaneous self:

This process is so closely interrelated with the previous one that they might almost be classed together. As material is given by the client, it is the therapist's function to help him recognize and clarify the emotions which he feels. In the rapport situation, where he is accepted rather than criticized, the individual is free to see himself without defensiveness, and gradually to recognize and admit his real self with its childish patterns, its aggressive feelings, and its ambivalences, as well as its mature impulses, and rationalized exterior. Often this recognition of self is achieved almost spontaneously, the therapist's only contribution having been to verbalize the feelings which are expressed in words or behavior or play activities. This process is very much akin to insight, except that it is on a basis of feeling, whereas the term insight is apt to have more of an intellectual connotation.

IV. The making of responsible choices:

Perhaps the sharpest difference between present day psychotherapy and earlier practice, is the degree to which the responsibility for the client's life is left in his own hands. The therapist at his best does not suggest, advise, or persuade. He does not assume responsibility for the client's decisions. Instead he encourages the individual, now more clearly aware of his true feelings, and with more acceptance of his total self, to take the responsibility for making new choices. Often hesitantly, often fearfully, the client does so, and is cheered and encouraged by the fact that he finds he can successfully take responsibility for himself, and can direct his energies toward new, self-chosen goals.

In actual therapeutic work there is something exciting and dramatic in these initial decisions, this growth toward independence, which visibly takes place in the therapeutic relationship. From the point of view of psychological theory, however, it is not so difficult to explain. It is a good example of "learning through doing." Whereas older therapies, relying on intellectual insight and personal influence, hoped that the patient might alter his ways outside of the treatment relationship, the newer therapy gives opportunity for the practice of independent choices, greater responsibility, while still supported by the rapport situation. Thus there is much greater "transfer of training" to other life situations.

V. The gaining of insight through assimilated interpretation:

The foundation of insight seems to be the emotional acceptance of self-mentioned under III. In addition, however, insight is often enriched by the therapist's interpretation of emotional patterns in the life of the individual which have not been recognized. Such interpretations, largely explanations of motives for behavior, serve no useful purpose, and may retard progress, if they are not accepted by the client. Hence, the use of the term "assimilated interpretation." Although this process has deep roots in Freudian psychoanalytic procedures, it is probably much less used than formerly. It is the one process described which may play very little, if any, part.

We undoubtedly owe much to Rank and Jung for the declining emphasis on insight alone. Insight plus responsible, self-directed choices toward new goals produces new and effective integration. Insight alone, as we see from some of the personal accounts of analysis in the Journal of Abnormal and Social Psychology, may leave the individual wiser, but little better able to cope with his situation.

VI. Growing into independence with support:

The final period of any therapeutic experience is the process of education or re-education which makes possible the effective continuance of the fundamental gains which have been made. In choosing new goals, the client may need new information which the therapist may supply or help him to obtain. In taking independent steps to cope with his adjustment problems, there will be discouragements and defeats, which the rapport situation helps to neutralize. In these new experiences there are fresh opportunities for the client to see himself even more clearly and to make use of the insight he has previously gained. If the initial aspects of therapy have been successful, this final period comes to a close quite naturally, with some feeling of loss on both sides to be sure, but with the client's feeling of assurance that he can now handle his situation alone.

These are suggested as the basic elements of psychotherapy as we now know it whether applied to nursery age children or gray-haired adults. While there is something very unsatisfactory in stripping therapy of the subtle nuances and dramatic elements which assuredly belong to it and presenting only the bare bones of therapeutic process, it is a necessary task if we are to make progress. The finest touches of artistry will not make counseling contacts helpful if they are basically unsound in principle. It is to attempt to give one formulation to these basic principles that this article has been written.

In closing, attention might be called to the research opportunities with which the therapeutic process bristles. There is the need of adequate records—stenographic, even phonographic—upon which comprehensive study may be based. There is the question of accessibility for therapy. Can we draw a line between those who would profit, and those who might be better helped by other treatment procedures?

There is the need for both imagination and research in the field of expression. Are the same basic feelings expressed in dreams, in play materials, in dramatic constructions, in verbalizations? There is need for much more study of the give and take of the interviewing process. How is expression encouraged, how may interpretations be made, how may the therapeutic progress be accelerated through the interview? There is the need for translating individual therapy into group procedures, to make it more widely helpful. There is the need for much more refined analysis of processes in therapy based on a study of complete records and formulated in terms of known psychological facts.

If clinical and applied psychology is to win the status it desires, if it is to find sound answers to the problems of human relationships which are so urgently needed in a distraught world, then it will need to promote much more study and effort than heretofore, in this dynamic field of therapy.

THE DEVELOPMENT OF INSIGHT
IN A COUNSELING RELATIONSHIP

IN dealing with adolescent and adult clients, one question which faces the worker—whether psychologist, case worker, psychiatrist, or educational counselor—is, "How may this individual come to an effective understanding of himself?" It is recognized that once the individual genuinely understands his behavior, and accepts that understanding, he is able to adopt a more realistic and satisfactory control of his actions, is less likely to hurt others to gain satisfactions, and in general can become more mature. But how to reach this goal?

This understanding of self we customarily call insight. We find rather general agreement that the achievement of insight is the keystone of the process of therapy. Whether we are dealing with a student who is maladjusted, or a marriage which is skidding toward failure, or a war neurosis, the essentials of a therapeutic experience seem to be the same. First comes the experience of release—the pouring out of feelings, the loosening of repressions, the unburdening of guilt, the lessening of tension. There follows, if progress is to be made, the understanding of self, the acceptance of one's impulses, the perception of relationships, which we classify under the term insight. Then, out of this more accurate view of the inner life, out of this new understanding of the web of personal adjustments, come new plans, new choices, new and more satisfying ways of meeting the realities with which the individual is faced. While each of these three steps is essential, and no one can take place without the other, the middle step, the achievement of insight, is a crucial one and deserves much more attention than it has had in the past.

In the counseling and the research on counseling which is being carried forward at Ohio State, we are gradually accumulating more information about this important aspect of psychotherapy. We are finding that in counseling relationships governed by a non-directive viewpoint, highly significant insights develop with a spontaneity and vigor which is astonishing [3]. We are also becoming more and more convinced, though, as yet research evidence is meagre, that such spontaneous insight is not characteristic of other counseling approaches. We find that the directive procedures which are characteristic of so much educational guidance do not produce insight of this sort. Our evidence would also point to the conclusion that spontaneous insight is a rare occurrence in the more interpretative approaches such as psychoanalysis. Consequently, it appears to be worthwhile to present both examples and research evidence regarding the achievement of self-understanding as we are seeing it.

Insight, as it is coming to be defined through our practical experience and research findings, involves such elements as (1) an acceptance of one's impulses and attitudes, good or bad, including attitudes previously repressed; (2) an understanding of the patterning of one's behavior, the perception of new relationships; (3) a fresh perception of reality made possible by this acceptance and understanding of the self; (4) the planning of new and more satisfying ways in which the self can adjust to reality. Since this definition grows out of examination of the data, not from armchair speculation, an attempt will be made to let the data speak for themselves.

Where problems are not too deep seated, simple and partial insights may come very quickly. A father, concerned about his ten-year-old daughter, is encouraged to talk out his attitudes, and arrives at these insightful reactions in a single interview [4].

Father: She's awful pokey—awful pokey. You just can't get her going. Of course, maybe it's been our fault. It's been easier to do things for her than to teach her to do them. She hasn't enough to do. She ought to have more responsibility.

Counselor: That's a splendid idea . . . You feel you haven't given her a chance to learn?

Father: Yes. She gets an allowance, but the trouble is she spends it. And then it comes time to go to the show and she hasn't any. And I haven't the heart—I give it to her. (Pause) Of course when I was a boy I didn't have any money at all—I had to earn everything.

Counselor: You think it would have been better if someone had given it to you?

Father: Well, it wouldn't have hurt. My parents could have . . . (Pause) I know I give in to her and she knows it, see?

This may seem like a minimum degree of insight. It could be briefly stated in these terms: "She should have more responsibility, but I don't give it to her because I feel sorry for myself as a boy." It is a simple insight, yet it is effective. Before the father leaves he says, in a hesitating manner, "I kinda think tomorrow morning when she wakes up she's going to find she has some things to do!" One year later the school principal, talking to the psychologist about this child, knowing nothing of the above, says, "Well, she seems better . . . . And the attitude of the parents seems different. They seem to be giving her more responsibility in various ways." This illustrates one of the points which I would like to make—that partial insights, spontaneously arrived at, are surprisingly effective in bringing about alteration of behavior.

Another illustration of such simple and partial insight might be given. A young bride has been troubled by guilt feelings about an experience previous to her marriage in which she had been intensely in love with a young man who regarded her as "just a passing fancy." She is troubled about keeping this experience from her husband. She talks out her attitudes in one contact, getting considerable release. In a second brief contact she shows how much insight she has gained.

"I guess I needed to talk to someone about it. I think I can see where I stand now. If I were to tell Nick it would merely mean that I was selfish. I would be telling him to help myself, not because of anything I feel I owe to him. It would be 'passing the buck' to him. I see now that it was merely an experience that hurt me—hurt my ego. It's only natural that I should feel queer about it. But that feeling queer is my own burden. Certainly it's unfair to pass it on to Nick. It would certainly be foolish of me to endanger our relationship, too. Time will cure my 'conditioning' to this very small unpleasant segment of my life—and my marital happiness will hasten this time. I already feel my perspective changing—the present looms larger and larger and the rest dwindles."

Here we find that the insight achieved involves a better acceptance of attitudes previously denied—the hurt to her ego—a clearer perception of the patterning and significance of her own desire to tell her husband, and finally a choice of a new method of handling the problem.

As might be expected, a working insight is not always so easily achieved. Much depends on the complexity of the problem, and the extent to which attitudes are repressed. In the case of an aviation cadet who was failing in his solo flights, counseling brought to light an intense and hitherto denied hatred for his unreasonably strict father. The gradual perception of a relationship between his attitude toward his father and his reactions during his flights covers several interviews.

Brief excerpts from the fifth, sixth, and tenth interviews will illustrate the development of this insight.

From fifth interview:

S. You know after the last interview I wondered what made me tell you the things that I did. Could it be possible that the instructor is a symbol of my father? Is that hatred coming back to blot my memory? Could that possibly be significant?

C. You wonder if perhaps the instructor might be a symbol of your father.

S. Yes, he was telling me what to do just like Dad always did. I fully intended to carry out the instructor's directions; I couldn't not want to do them. Maybe I forgot because I thought of Dad and wanted to forget.

From the sixth interview:

S. On the basis of what we've done thus far the instructor may have been considered in the role of my father and as he was telling me what to do I probably didn't want to because I thought of him as my father—but I don't know—I'm not sure.

C. You're not absolutely sure that that's the answer to your problem.

S. I'm not positive but that's what it seems to be at the present time. If you said it was I would know it. Then recognizing that fact, I wouldn't be bothered in the plane any more.

C. If I should say that was the solution to your problem and you didn't thoroughly believe it yourself, that wouldn't do much good, would it? Or if I told you that wasn't the solution to your problem, and you thought that perhaps it was, then my telling you wouldn't do a bit of good either.

S. (Smiling) I see your point. I guess you're right.

From the tenth interview:

The cadet tells of a recent failure to do well. The counselor recognizes his feeling.

C. You didn't follow his instructions up in the air even when he was telling you.

S. It seems that way. If you could apply that to other maneuvers it might be. I really want to fly though. Maybe that's why I haven't done so well—a dislike to follow directions. Gee, that's pretty well tangled up. Let me try and draw a parallel there. My instructor is to my father as my instructor's directions are to my father's directions. Even though I thought I wanted to, I really didn't want to.

C. You feel there's a parallel to your father's and instructor's directions.

S. I wanted to fly badly. That may be the block. That's probably the answer to the question. I guess I didn't have it formulated before I came here today, but I sure do now.

C. You feel that may be at the center of your problem.

S. That's right. Flying is grand. By George, why did I have to get an instructor that reminded me of father? If I got an easy instructor all the way through would it have been easier? There's a good possibility I would have been the best in the group.

In this material the insight which is gained is primarily a new perception of relationships between past repressed attitudes and present experiences. It should be pointed out that neither in this case, nor in any of the cases cited in this paper, has the counselor ever suggested these insights in any way. The counseling has been non-directive, with the counselor reflecting, in an understanding fashion, the attitudes and feelings expressed. The understanding of self springs from the client, not from the counselor.

In other instances the insight consists largely of an acceptance of the denied portions of the self. Illustrations of this type of insight may be taken from the case of Mrs. S., a young, highly educated mother, who comes for assistance because she is having trouble with her child and is losing the affection of her husband. Some of the points at which she comes face to face with her own feelings may be given. First she faces her basic rejection of her child.

Mrs. S. I'm afraid I'd have to say this of myself, I really didn't want Buddy. We were married two years, and I had a job. My husband didn't want me to work. We thought children would be the best solution. We felt social pressure too. With the birth rate up in the lower groups, college graduates should have children. In a limited way we were emotionally interested in him, but not deeply. And I've never adjusted to having him! It's terrible to say this!

Later she sees the relationship of this rejection, and of her difficulty with her husband, to Buddy's behavior.

Mrs. S. He senses the tension in us, lacks security. That probably explains it all. I used to put myself into working for social causes. Now I've given myself all to my husband, none to Buddy. I pat him and tell him I love him, but I wonder if he doesn't know.

C. You feel perhaps he realizes you don't love him much.

Mrs. S. Say not till now. But with the situation as it is—how will it come?

C. You want to love him.

Mrs. S. Yes, very much. I'm not just coldblooded.

At another point she begins to accept the role of being a woman, rather than merely an intellectual. Talking about her husband, she says:

Mrs. S. I spend my time worrying about him, discussing with him his feelings and emotions. Instead I should take an interest in myself, my clothes, my hair. I've never been that sort of person—I hate to fuss with my hair. I shouldn't say that—after I'm through, and look in the mirror, I like myself better. That's the first time I've thought of it that way.

C. Instead of being tense about him, you feel you should take an interest in yourself, and you find that doing that, like fussing with your hair, is not as foreign to your nature as you thought.

Mrs. S. Yes. I have more hope now than I have felt to this moment.

In regard to her relationship to her husband, this woman also gains much insight in which she sees the problem in a new frame of reference, and also decides what she can do about it.

Mrs. S. I'm more firmly convinced than ever that what I have to look at is myself, rather than Bill, do something about my own faults and shortcomings. I thought a lot about it last night; I realized a person can only be responsible for oneself, not for the other person's feelings and emotions. I wasn't treating him as an individual—my emotional involvement makes that hard. I tried to think and feel for him, take over his problem and work it through for him.

C. Now you feel you can be responsible for yourself, and can let him be responsible for himself.

Mrs. S. Yes. Things may break down, but we can build them up again.

C. While things may not go smoothly, you feel more basic security.

Mrs. S. Yes. I've got to look to myself, to see how I'm dressing and behaving with him.

C. You feel those are your responsibility.

Mrs. S. Yes. And the children—I'm not excusing myself about them. I thought it was impossible for anyone to take care of a house, and herself, and find time to play with the children, but I think now I can. I'd assumed some things were impossible, but they were not.

In these excerpts, being able to accept as a part of herself her rejecting attitudes, and her desire to be a woman, enables her to achieve a more detached and realistic attitude toward the reality of her husband and his behavior. It also frees her to choose new patterns of reaction.

In the instances which have been given the insights which were achieved were relatively simple, though definitely significant. In some cases insights are much more involved, and the achievement of them is a more gradual process. A series of excerpts from the case of Alfred will indicate something of the richness which this insight process may have. Alfred was a very withdrawn student, the reclusive sort who was living largely in fantasy when he first came in. The possibility of a schizophrenic break seemed very real. There were twenty interviews, and during that period he altered in a most striking fashion in his behavior and attitudes. He became independent and socially adjusted, indeed something of a social leader. His adjustment has been further tested by two years in the army, to which he has reacted very well. There are in his case many threads of insight which would be intriguing to follow. One which has been selected is his gradual achievement of understanding of his daydreaming. His gropings toward this insight are a fascinating process to watch. It is unfortunate that only brief excerpts can be given from the phonographic recordings of the contacts.

In the seventh interview: Alfred first shows a real understanding of the fact that his daydreaming was compensatory.

Alfred. I always had the idea that I would make up for a lot of the things I didn't do—like being an Edison or a Lincoln some day. Yet I never did enjoy the real happiness that kids were having at the present time. I always kidded myself along by thinking that 'I'm going to be a great man someday'—And when you get to college, and really find out how many brilliant people there are you realize you've been kidding yourself. You certainly never could become important if you were to go on in the past, instead of concentrating and studying and everything. I think maybe if I could be as happy as this I could amount to something— probably not an Edison or Lincoln, but I could hold a position. It would certainly be through an entirely different set of plans than I planned on the other way of doing it.

In the tenth interview he brings out more forcibly how much the fantasy meant to him, and how difficult has been the process of bringing it into the full light of consciousness.

Alfred. So anyway I do believe coming over here is helping me, because these things don't bother me as much as they used to. And I used to carry them around with me. For instance, that daydreaming. Boy, it just about killed me the first time I tried to tell that to anybody, but I suppose that if I tell it about twenty-five times I'll really begin to laugh at it.

In the eleventh interview he expands the insight gained. He is able to face the fact that the satisfactions of fantasy existed not only in the past, but even during the initial stages of counseling. He also faces frankly the fact that his fantasy goals are impossible.

Alfred. I just used to comfort myself at school by telling myself that I would be a very famous person some day, and I didn't just say that as a sort of compromise, I actually believed that that was right, and even when I was coming here I still did think that. I remember one time I said to myself, 'If I were happy I would be another Abe Lincoln,' but if your mind is really normal and out in the world, you realize how really big the world is and you realize that maybe you aren't going to accomplish as much as you want.

In the fourteenth interview Alfred makes the final link in this chain of insight when he becomes genuinely willing to face and accept the prospect of being only an average person, in the real world, rather than a great person in a fantasy world of his own making.

Alfred. I might desire to be an awfully great person, but really just to be average and to be normal is something to be very appreciative of, because I was thinking it could very easily be that I could grow up to be a bum. I was watching some of the newsies, men about 35 or 40, selling their papers, and I thought, 'Gee, just to be average really isn't such a little thing.' For a man to have a respected position, he really doesn't need to be known even in his own community as a great figure, but to be average is really a very high position compared with how low a person could fall in the opposite direction where he would be a bum.

In these excerpts we see Alfred openly accepting his fantasies, and able to bring them fully into consciousness, recognizing that they are compensatory, recognizing that he has used them as a means of satisfaction right up to the present, perceiving the difference between fantasy satisfactions and the less glamorous but more substantial satisfactions of real goals, and finally accepting a realistic goal as his own. This is a rich, deep, and thoroughly effective instance of spontaneous insight.

In this same case there is still another thread of insight which is worthy of our attention. He was, as has been mentioned, a very withdrawn young man, with no satisfying contacts of a social nature, standing on the brink of creating his own private world in the form of a psychosis. A few of his statements, as he comes to see himself more clearly in this respect, will both illustrate the achievement of insight, and reveal the way the world looks to a highly reclusive individual. During the seventh interview he indicates something of his isolation, and the dawning realization that he might be able to deal with it.

Alfred. It's like a curtain in a theatre, something that shuts me off from the players in the rest of the play. Just completely isolates me. Until I pull that curtain away and look at myself as being one of the players the same as anyone else, I won't be able to get very far. At times when I really get to looking at these things the way I should, I wonder why I don't jump in and get in the stream of life.

In the eleventh interview he begins to see this isolation as being partially in the past, giving a vivid picture of the way he felt. He also recognizes that he is changing, living more in a world of social reality.

Alfred. I just withdrew a little more each year until things had gotten to a point that around Christmas time I started to wonder for fear I was the only person that was alive. I must have gotten away from the present world that much, that everything just kind of disappeared, kinda, and I felt as if I were standing on a hill all alone or something, and everything was gone, and here I was all alone. But the more I start going back in the group, why—I know the other day I was thinking about something, I don't know, I had my mind on something else, and I suddenly got the idea, 'Well, how in the world could I have gotten the idea that I was the only person existing. Here this person is every bit the same as I am.'

As might be supposed, it is not an easy matter to face all these deep problems within the self, and reorient to new goals, yet growth was steadily made during the interviews. In the sixteenth interview Alfred gives a picture of the two opposing forces within himself, the desire for growth and the desire to withdraw from life. His description of the constructive turmoil into which his life has been thrown has the genuine literary quality which only accompanies a struggle to say deeply significant things.

Alfred. I certainly think in a way the problem is a lot clearer than a while ago, yet—maybe—It's like the ice breaking up on a pond in the spring, it's—while things are a lot nearer to—While the pond is a lot nearer to being nothing but clear water, yet things are much more unstable now, possibly, than when the pond was covered over with ice. What I'm trying to bring out is that I seem to be so much in a terrible fog all of the time lately, but I do feel a lot better off than I was before, because then I didn't even realize what was the matter. But maybe all this fog and so-called trouble is due to the fact of two opposing forces in me now. You know it's not really a case of just letting one be superior, but it's kinda breaking up and reorganizing that's going on now that makes things seem so doubly bad. So maybe I'm better off than I think.

The person who is skilled in therapy will realize that this is a deep and genuine insight, and will not be surprised that in the next interview Alfred made a definite decision to obtain a job as junior counselor in a summer camp, a step he had contemplated before, but about which he had been unable to come to a clear decision.

In this second train of insightful thinking, which could be illustrated with many other examples from the recordings, Alfred sees clearly his icebound, frozen, isolated personality, and comes to see also the attractiveness of life in a social, real, world. Though he also perceives the pain and difficulty of such a radical reorganization of life, he is able to face this and to take steps in the direction of social life and social responsibility.

As may have been noted, these spontaneous insights, wrought out of the individual's struggle to see himself more clearly, have a depth and a sincerity and an individual quality which are quite lacking in attempts on the part of the counselor to "give" the client insight. This is the person seen from within, rather than without, and the difference is very striking. As an illustration of the attempt to give insight, a portion may be taken from an electrically recorded psychoanalysis, conducted by a reputable psychoanalyst. This example could be duplicated hundreds of times in the course of the 424 interviews of the analysis.

The patient, a schizophrenic young man, has been telling, in the fourth interview, about vaguely guilty feelings which he had while in the cafeteria, and the thought that if he did not eat much for lunch, he could later go to the candy counter, but then remarks that these ideas are foolish. The interview continues:

Analyst. What does eating candy make you think of?

Patient. Home, right away now. That's what it means.

Analyst. And what does home make you think of?

Patient. My mother.

Analyst. And what does your mother make you think of?

Patient. Oh, children, babies. Those ideas are put in my head. I don't know. I've got those thoughts again in my head.

Analyst. Yes. And as you think of babies, what comes into your mind?

Patient. Girls, I guess. Barbara Royce.

Analyst. Barbara Royce?

Patient. Yes. (very long pause).

Analyst. You see, you have guilt about Barbara Royce. You undoubtedly have sex feelings about her and something within yourself has been trying to convince you that this is wrong. That same part of your personality is making you feel guilty about eating, about going down to the cafeteria, about asking for a second course, about eating candy. You see, it connects right up with the thoughts that come, that somehow you—one part of you is trying to make you believe that all of that is wrong. Well, we know it isn't. (Pause) Why shouldn't you feel that way toward girls?

Patient. Well, I don't see any reason why I shouldn't. That's just a— Well, it's all right. (Long pause.)

Here it seems all too clear that any seeing of relationships, any perception of pattern, is in the mind of the analyst, not in the mind of the patient. The nearest he comes to accepting his own feelings is a passive acceptance of the analyst's attitude, by saying, "Well, it's all right." This is pale indeed alongside of the spontaneous insights which we have been examining. It lacks any of the internal conviction which they carry. It shows how weak are attempts to give insight, when compared with the client's achievement of insight.

Our knowledge regarding insight comes not only from such examples as have been given, but from research studies which have been made. Three of these investigations have findings pertinent to the topic of insight. Snyder [5] has made an objective study of the characteristics of nondirective counseling in six complete counseling cases. He devised an objective list of 38 carefully defined categories and classified each of the nearly 10,000 client and counselor responses into one of these categories, thus making possible a statistical study of the counseling process. Raimy [2] has studied the changing concepts of the self which the individual exhibits in counseling. His study is based on 14 recorded cases. Curran [1] has made an exhaustive analysis of the case of Alfred, with particular reference to the problem of insight. From these three studies certain findings in regard to self-understanding in non-directive counseling may be briefly stated, with the source in parenthesis.

1. Insight primarily follows outpourings of material with a negative emotional content, colored by such attitudes as hostility, self criticism, and hopelessness. (Curran, 1.)

2. Insightful responses are most likely to follow immediately upon counselor responses of simple acceptance. They tend not to follow interpretation, persuasion, or other directive counselor responses. (Snyder, 5.)

3. An important aspect of insight is the seeing of relationships between issues heretofore regarded as unrelated.(Curran, 1.)

4. Another important aspect of insight is the alteration of concepts of the self. Individuals who come for counseling tend to see themselves in a strongly negative light as worthless, bad, inferior, etc. As insight is gained and the self is accepted, the self-concept is reorganized and a strong positive valuation is placed on it. The individual sees himself in much more positive terms. (Raimy, 2.)

5. As insight is gained into given problems or issues, those problems tend to drop out of the client's conversation. (Curran, 1.)

6. Insight and the making of independent plans and decisions both constitute a very small fraction of the client's conversation at the outset of counseling, but rise to become a significant part of the concluding interviews. These two categories taken together constitute 12.5 per cent of the client responses in initial interviews, 30.5 per cent of the middle interviews, and 42.5 per cent of the final counseling interviews. (Snyder, 5.)

With the evidence thus far given, indicating that spontaneous insights do occur in non-directive counseling, that they exhibit themselves in a variety of ways, and that they are significant in altering the client's concept of himself and his way of behaving, it becomes important to ask ourselves, under what conditions is this spontaneous insight most likely to be achieved?

A careful examination of a growing body of data brings one to the conclusion that there is one primary principle operative. When the client is freed from all need of being in any way defensive, spontaneous insight comes bubbling through into consciousness. When the client is talking through his problems in an atmosphere in which all his attitudes are genuinely understood and accepted, and in which there is nothing to arouse his desire to protect himself, insight develops.

Some workers will feel disappointed in the simplicity of this conclusion. They will feel that they have always dealt with clients in an accepting fashion. The fact is however that most of the procedures actually used in counseling contacts are such as to make clients defensive. This is clearly shown by our study of recorded interviews. It is not enough for the worker to have an accepting attitude, though this is important. The techniques used must also be such that defensiveness will not be aroused. Let us look at some of the methods actually employed by most workers.

Questions, for example, constitute one of the methods most frequently used in counseling. They may be simple questions such as, "When was that?" "Did he like it?" Or they may constitute an attempt to get deeper into attitudes expressed by asking, "Why did you feel that way about it?" "Why did you think that was bad?" "Why do you think these things happen?" Or questions may be of a highly probing nature, "What did you think about your mother?" "Will you behave next time the way you did this time?" In varying degrees all these questions arouse the psychological defenses of the client. There is always the fear that the questions may go too far, may uncover the attitudes which the client is afraid to reveal even to himself. Snyder's study showed that counselor questions tend to be followed frequently by rejection of the question by the client.

Evaluative responses are another familiar aspect of counseling. We have learned long ago that negative evaluations—comments which imply criticism, which question motives, which pass judgment on the client—tend to freeze the situation, and to make spontaneous expression difficult. We have not sufficiently learned that reassurance, agreement, and commendation have the same effect to a lesser degree. "I agree with, you," "You're certainly right," "You've done very well," "You don't need to feel guilty about that," are the sort of well-intentioned comments which actually make it more difficult for the client to bring contradictory attitudes into the relationship. They show that the counselor is passing judgment on the client. These particular attitudes are judged favorably but the client fears that there may be attitudes which will be judged unfavorably, and hence is unable to bring his thinking fully into the interview.

Advice and suggestions are, we know, freely given even by those who protest strongly that they do not wish to guide the client's life. "Of course you will want to make your own decision, but I think you might try . . ." is one of the many subtle ways by which we introduce our own solutions to the client's problems. Such procedures cut off free expression. In two ways they make the client defensive. If he brings out deeper attitudes it would seem to imply that the counselor had not solved the problem. It would also bring the possibility that the counselor would try to solve these deeper problems in ways which the client did not want.

Interpretation of the client to himself is a technique used somewhat by psychologists and social workers, and very heavily by psychiatrists and analysts. The more shrewd the interpretation, the more it hits the mark, the greater the defensiveness it arouses, unless the client has already reached that point of insight himself. Snyder found that interpretation, even when made by skilled counselors, is most likely to be followed by client responses which deny the interpretation. The client is thrown on the defensive.

To sum it up, most of the procedures which we customarily use in counseling tend to put the client subtly on his guard. As we analyze our psychotherapeutic contacts there are only two techniques which are actually in accord with the accepting viewpoint which most workers profess. These are simple acceptance— "Yes," "M-hm," "I understand"—and recognition and clarification of feeling. The first needs no explanation, but there is no doubt that it serves an important part in developing a permissive atmosphere where the client can discover insight.

The procedure of recognizing and clarifying attitudes is one which also has a deceptive simplicity. It consists in mirroring, reflecting for the client the feelings he has been expressing, often more clearly than he has been able to do for himself. Two examples might be given. The first one is a very simple reflection of a straightforward attitude, taken from the case of the aviation cadet mentioned earlier.

Cadet. I should have soloed long ago. And here is something. Before I joined the Navy I was an overhead electrical crane operator, and that takes depth perception, coordination, and alertness; and I'm positive that I can apply that to my flying.

Counselor. You feel that your training as a crane operator should help you in your flying.

Cadet. That's right And here's something else . . .

This simple recognition of feeling serves the purpose of making expression of attitude easy, and of interposing nothing which will make the client in any way defensive. It makes him feel that he is understood, and enables him to go on to another area of emotionalized attitude, until gradually he has worked into the deeper and really significant realms.

Responses which might be termed clarification serve a further purpose of assisting the client to understand himself, but without any trace of an approach which would arouse defensiveness. A brief example from a case in which the man was disturbed over his tendency to gamble excessively will illustrate this point.

Mr. R. One thing I have thought of vaguely, that might be the cause of everything; I have had the props knocked out from under me so many times since I went into business. After I got out of the University I went into business in L—, and had a good practice there, but my family didn't want me to stay there. They kept after me until I gave it up and came home. I worked for my father then, and had just gotten up to a decent job when I was let out for no particular reason. Next time I set up a lease that was profitable, and just at the time when I was about ready to profit from it, they cancelled the lease.

Counselor. You feel that the breaks have been against you.

Here the counselor's response puts briefly, and in clearer form, the underlying attitude which the client has been expressing. It is as such recognition and clarification of feeling frees the client from all need for defense, since it never in any way attacks the ego, that expression becomes freer, deeper attitudes are brought forth, and insights are developed. The justification for the development of these nondirective attitudes, and the skills which implement them, lie in the results which they bring.

This material has certain clear implications for the worker who deals with maladjusted clients in need of help. If deeper degrees of insight are deemed desirable, if it is important that the client reorganize his concept of himself, if he needs to find fresh and more satisfying ways of dealing with his problem, then the worker will increase the likelihood of this by adopting certain view points and procedures. The worker will need to cultivate a tolerant, accepting attitude which quite genuinely accepts the individual as he is. Furthermore the worker will need to utilize in the counseling situation only those techniques, which prevent defensiveness from arising. Aside from simple acceptance, the major technique is that of mirroring for the client the emotionalized attitude which he is expressing. Snyder found that these two types of responses constituted nearly 75 per cent of the counselor's statements in non-directive counseling. Their use and the counselor's accepting attitude are undoubtedly the primary reason for the development of the spontaneous insights which have been discussed, insights which deeply alter the client's way of living.

SUMMARY

1. It has been found that in counseling situations of a nondirective character, new perceptions and understandings of self develop in spontaneous fashion.

2. These insights are of various types, some relatively simple, some highly complex and going to the root of the behavior patterns of the individual.

3. Research shows that these insights develop gradually in a non-directive counseling situation and mount to a peak toward the conclusion of the counseling experience. They follow free expression of negative emotion. They are closely connected with a positive change in the self concept. They are accompanied or followed by plans and decisions which involve the alteration of behavior.

4. Insights are not likely to follow counselor procedures "which evaluate, question, probe, advise or interpret. They are likely to develop if the counselor uses responses which are accepting and clarifying. Procedures which make defensiveness on the part of the client completely unnecessary, but which make the client feel that lie is deeply understood, are most successful.

REFERENCES

1. Curran, Chas. A. An Analysis of a Process of Therapy Through Counseling and its Implications for a Philosophy of Personality. Unpublished Ph.D. thesis, the Ohio State University, Columbus, Ohio, 1944.

2. Raimy, Victor C. The Self-Concept as a Factor in Counseling and Personality Organization. Unpublished Ph.D. thesis, the Ohio State University, Columbus, Ohio, 1943.
3. Rogers, Carl R. Counseling and Psychotherapy Boston: Houghton Mifflin, 1942.
4. Sargent, Helen. "Non-directive Counseling Applied to a Single Interview," JOURNAL OF CONSULTING PSYCHOLOGY, 1943, 7: 186.
5. Snyder, Wm. U. An Investigation of the Nature of Non-Directive Psychotherapy. Unpublished Ph.D. thesis, The Ohio State University, Columbus, Ohio, 1943. A condensation of this thesis is shortly to be published in the Journal of General Psychology.

www.ingramcontent.com/pod-product-compliance
Lightning Source LLC
Chambersburg PA
CBHW022105020426
42335CB00012B/842